This book belongs to

Lynn Weaver   Christmas 1997
from Grandmother +
Grandad

The Big Book of
All-Time Favorite Bible Stories

First Inspirational Press edition published in 1997.

Inspirational Press
A division of BBS Publishing Corporation
386 Park Avenue South
New York, NY 10016

Inspirational Press is a registered trademark of BBS Publishing Corporation.

Published by arrangement with Educational Publishing Concepts, Inc.

Library of Congress Catalog Card Number: 97-71141

ISBN: 0-88486-183-X

Printed in China

The Big Book of
All-Time Favorite Bible Stories

V. Gilbert Beers
Ronald A. Beers

Illustrated by
Daniel J. Hochstatter

An Inspirational Press Book
for Children

A Word to Parents

We all need heroes, people who are role models for us, to show us how to live. Children especially look for heroes to leave tracks in life's sands so they can follow.

Too often, people today seek their heroes among the famous people—movie or TV stars, sports personalities, and rock singers. A few of these may leave good footprints for your children to follow, but many do not. So where can you help your children find their heroes? What kind of people should your children seek as role models?

Of course we want our children to follow our ways as parents or teachers. Many do. But they WILL seek other heroes, too. But where?

Some of the truly great heroes of life are found in the Bible. For generations parents have guided their children into the great Bible stories to search for the footprints left by God's great heroes and to encourage their children to walk in those footprints.

Likewise, parents for generations have pointed to the villains mentioned in the great Bible stories, those who have left the wrong footprints in life's sands, and parents have encouraged their children NOT to follow their example.

This is a BIG book of Bible heroes and villains, stories of people who have been remembered by parents and children of many generations. Encourage your children to seek out the true heroes and walk in their footprints as they walked with God. Likewise, help your children to discern, and avoid, the footprints left by those who walked another way.

V. Gilbert Beers & Ronald A. Beers

The Big Book of All-Time Favorite Bible Stories

Stories from the Old Testament

Stories from the New Testament

God Creates a Wonderful World

In the beginning, when God began to create the heavens and earth, the earth had no shape. God's Spirit hovered over these dark waters. "Let there be light!" God said. Light appeared, and God divided the light from darkness. He called the light "day" and the darkness "night." Thus ended the first day.

"Let the sky and oceans separate," God said. The sky and oceans took form. Thus ended the second day.

"Let the oceans and the dry land separate," God said. God called the dry land "earth" and the oceans "seas." God was pleased. He also caused grass and plants to grow and trees to appear with seeds. This happened on the third day.

On the fourth day God made the sun, the moon, and the stars. The sun shone by day and the moon and stars at night. God was pleased with this work.

God made fish and birds on the fifth day.

On the sixth day He made all kinds of living creatures. He was pleased with all this, too. On the sixth day God also made a man and a woman. The man was Adam. Adam named the woman Eve.

God put the man and woman in a beautiful garden named Eden. They were supposed to take care of the garden and the animals for God. When God finished all He had done, He rested on the seventh day. He was pleased with His work, and He was pleased with this special day for rest. God called this day holy for it was the day He rested from all His work.

Adam and Eve Sin

When God put Adam and Eve in the garden of Eden He gave them everything they needed. They could eat every kind of fruit except one. "You must not eat this fruit," God told them. "If you do, you will die."

One day a serpent said to Eve, "You will not die if you eat this fruit. Your eyes will be opened, and you will know the difference between good and evil."

Eve listened to the serpent. The fruit looked so good that she ate some. She even gave some to Adam to eat. Suddenly they both realized that they were not wearing clothes. They were ashamed and made aprons of fig leaves to cover themselves.

That evening, Adam and Eve heard God walking in the garden. They hid. "Why are you hiding?" God asked.

Then Adam and Eve told God what had happened. "You must crawl on your belly in the dust," God told the serpent. "You and the woman's children will fear one another."

"You will have pain and suffering when you have children," God told Eve. Then He told Adam, "You must work hard and sweat to earn your living. When you die, your body will go back into the ground from which I made it."

God also made Adam and Eve leave the garden of Eden. He put mighty angels at the entrance to the garden to keep them out and a flaming sword to keep them from eating from the tree of life. If they ate that fruit, they would live forever, but not the way God wanted them to live.

So the happy days in the garden of Eden were over.

Cain Kills Abel

Adam and Eve had two sons, Cain and Abel. When they grew up Cain became a farmer and Abel became a shepherd. Each brought offerings to God. Abel brought meat from his lambs while Cain brought grain. God liked Abel's offering, but not Cain's. This made Cain angry. His face grew ugly with anger.

"Why are you angry, and why do you look that way?" God asked Cain. "Obey Me and you will be happy. If you don't, you will let sin hurt you."

But Cain grew more angry. He became jealous of his brother Abel. One day he asked Abel to go for a walk with him in the fields. There he attacked Abel and killed him.

God came to Cain and asked him, "Where is your brother Abel?"

"How should I know?" Cain demanded. "Must I watch over him?"

But the Lord told Cain, "Your brother's blood cries out from the ground. You must leave this place and never come back. It will never grow crops for you again. You must wander from place to place on the earth."

"But people will try to kill me," said Cain.

"If they do, they will be punished," God told him. So God put a mark on Cain so people would know who he was. They would know that they should not hurt him. And God sent Cain away to another land.

Noah and the Great Flood

As time passed, people sinned more than ever. God saw all this evil and was sorry that He had made these people. At last He said, "I will take these people from the face of the earth, along with their living creatures."

But Noah was a man who pleased God. So God spoke to Noah and told him what He would do. "I will destroy all people except you and your family," He said. "You must make a big boat and put each kind of animal and bird on it."

Noah listened carefully and did exactly what God told him. He worked for many years to build the big boat. Then he put each kind of animal and bird on it. One day God closed the door of the big boat, the ark. Then He caused it to rain for 40 days and 40 nights.

A great flood of water swept over the earth and all other people and animals were drowned. Only Noah and his family, and the animals and birds on the ark were saved.

Noah and his family lived on this ark for a long time until the water of the flood disappeared. At last they could open the door and go out on dry land again.

Noah made an altar of stones and burned some meat on it. That was his way of saying thank you to God for saving him and his family. Then God put a beautiful rainbow in the sky. It was a special promise from God. "I will never destroy all people and animals with a great flood again," God promised Noah.

The Tower of Babel

Long, long ago everyone on earth spoke the same language. Nobody knows for sure what that language was. But it was not English or German or Spanish. It was probably not any other language that people speak today.

Many people moved to a large plain in the land of Babylonia. There they built a great city. In that city they began to build a tower that would reach up to the sky. "This tower will bring us together and make us look powerful and important," the people said. "It will keep us from scattering over the earth." So the people made hundreds of bricks. Then they began to build the tower.

But God did not like this tower. He did not like what they were trying to do with it.

"If they are doing all this now, what will they do later?" God wondered. "I will make them speak different languages. Then they won't understand one another."

God knew that the people who spoke the same language would live together. Those who spoke different languages would move away because they could not understand one another. So that was the way God scattered the people over the earth. The city was not finished. The tower was not finished. The city became known as Babel. The name meant "confusion." Don't you think there must have been a lot of confusion when people began speaking different languages? Don't you think there must have been a lot of confusion when people began moving from Babel?

Abram Moves to a New Land

When God scattered people from Babel, the people went to live in different cities. Some went to a place called Ur. There they lived and had sons, grandsons, and great-grandsons. Years later a man named Terah grew up there. He had three sons named Abram, Nahor, and Haran.

Abram married Sarai, but they could not have children. So when Abram's brother Haran died, Abram and Sarai raised Haran's young son Lot.

One day the family decided to move to the land of Canaan, far to the west of their home at Ur. So Terah, Abram, Sarai, Lot, and other family members packed all their things together and left their homes. They drove their flocks and herds with them, heading toward the new land.

But along the way, the family stopped at a city named Haran. While there, Terah died. He was a very old man.

Then one day God spoke to Abram. "Leave your relatives here, and go on to Canaan," God told Abram. "I will cause you to become the father of a great nation. I will bless those who bless you and curse those who curse you."

So Abram did what God told him to do. At the age of seventy-five, he took his wife, Sarai, and his nephew Lot and all his animals and things and went on to Canaan.

When the family arrived in Canaan, at a place called Shechem, they set up their tents beside a large oak tree at Moreh.

God appeared to Abram again and told him, "I will give this land to your descendants." Then Abram built an altar there in memory of God's visit.

Abram moved on south of there, stopping for a while near Bethel and Ai. Once more he made an altar to God and prayed to Him there.

Abram and Lot Part

As the years passed Abram became a rich man. He had lots of gold and silver. He had many animals and servants. Abram must have helped his nephew Lot, because Lot became rich. He had many animals and servants, too.

But trouble came. There wasn't enough pasture for all these animals. Before long Lot's servants and Abram's servants began to quarrel. They shouldn't have been quarreling among themselves, of course. They were already in danger because of the tribes that lived nearby, the Canaanites and the Perizzites.

Abram decided to talk with Lot about this. "We can't let our families quarrel like this," he said. "The neighbors must not see us divided. Choose the land you want and I will take what is left. If you want this piece, I will take that piece. If you want that piece, I will take this piece."

At that time, before Sodom and Gomorrah were destroyed, the best land was along the Jordan River. It was like the Garden of Eden, or the beautiful land near Zoar in Egypt.

So Lot chose this land, which was the best, for himself, and moved there. Abram moved on the land that was left.

But Abram must have been sad to see his nephew Lot move near the wicked city of Sodom. The people who lived there were more wicked than the other neighbors and sinned much against God.

God Makes a Covenant with Abraham

When Abram was ninety-nine years old, God talked to him one day. "Walk before Me and live the way you should," God told Abram. "I will agree to make you into a great nation. You will even be the father of many nations."

Abram fell with his face down in the dust as God talked. "I am changing your name," God told Abram. "I will call you Abraham. This means 'father of nations.'

"I will keep this agreement through many years," God told Abraham. "I will give all this land to you and your descendants forever. And I will be your God. Your part of the agreement is to walk before Me." Then God talked with Abraham about his wife. "Her name is now Sarah," God said. That meant "mother of nations."

God surprised Abraham by telling him that he and Sarah would have a baby boy. Abraham laughed when he heard this. "I will have a baby when I am a hundred years old?" he said. "And Sarah will have a baby when she is ninety?"

"You will name him Isaac," God told Abraham. "My agreement will continue through him. He will be born about this time next year." The agreement that God made with Abraham is called a covenant. It was an important promise that would never be broken.

Angels Visit Abraham's Tent

One hot afternoon Abraham was sitting by his tent at Mamre. Suddenly he saw three men coming toward him through the grove of terebinth trees. Abraham stood up and went out to meet them. He did not know that they were angels. They all looked like men.

"Stay here and rest in the shade of this tree. I will get water to wash your feet and something for you to eat. This will help you rest before you go on your way."

"We will stay and let you do what you say," the angels said.

Soon Abraham, Sarah, and the servants were hurrying here and there, getting food ready.

"Where is Sarah?" the angels asked.

"Inside the tent," Abraham answered.

"Next year you and Sarah will have a son," one of them said. This was actually God talking to Abraham, but Abraham did not know who He was.

Sarah laughed when she heard this. She was too old have a baby.

"Why did Sarah laugh?" God asked Abraham. "Is anything too hard for Me? Next year you will have a baby!"

Sarah was afraid now. "I didn't laugh," she said. Both Abraham and Sarah must have known by now that this was God talking to them.

At last God went on His way and Abraham went back into his tent. Abraham knew for sure that he and Sarah would have a baby boy by next year.

The Destruction of Sodom

After the angels talked with Abraham, they went on their way to Sodom. That evening they arrived at the gate of the city, where Lot was sitting. Lot invited these men to his house and fed them a wonderful meal.

"Get your relatives out of this city," the angels warned Lot. "We will destroy the city and all who are in it because they are so wicked. Hurry!" Lot talked with his sons-in-law, but they thought he was joking and refused to leave. "Then take your wife and daughters and get out of here!" the angels urged.

Lot didn't seem to understand how urgent it was so he didn't hurry. At last the angels grabbed their hands and led Lot and his wife and daughters out of the city.

"Now run for your lives!" they urged. "Run to the mountains and don't look back."

"Please don't send me to the mountains," Lot argued. "Let us go to that little city over there to live." The angels would not argue any more. They let Lot and his family go to the little city called Zoar. The sun was just coming up when Lot and his family reached Zoar. Then God sent fire and brimstone down on Sodom and Gomorrah. They were completely destroyed because of their wickedness.

Lot's wife did not obey God, though, for she looked back. When she did, she became a pillar of salt.

That morning Abraham looked toward Sodom and Gomorrah. He must have felt sad as he saw the smoke. But God had kept Lot safe.

Hagar and Ishmael Are Sent Away

The time came for Abraham and Sarah to have a baby boy, as God had promised. They named him Isaac, as God told them to do.

Some time later Abraham gave a party for Isaac. Sarah was there, of course. So were Hagar and Ishmael.

Years before, Abraham and Sarah had given up hope that they would have a son because they were very old. So they arranged for Hagar to have a son for Sarah.

Through the years Sarah had treated Ishmael as her own son. But now she had her own son, Isaac.

Suddenly, Sarah noticed Ishmael teasing young Isaac at the party. She grew angry and turned to Abraham.

"Get that slave girl and her son out of here," she demanded. "He will not have any of your things."

Abraham was upset when he heard this. Ishmael was his son too.

But God spoke to Abraham. "You must not be upset," He said. "Do what Sarah says."

So Abraham gave Hagar and Ishmael some food and water and sent them into the wilderness near Beersheba. When the water was gone, Hagar began to cry. She was sure that Ishmael would die. But God showed her a well nearby.

Hagar and Ishmael continued to live in the wilderness.

They never went back to live with Abraham and Sarah. But God blessed them. He promised Hagar that Ishmael would become the head of a great nation.

Abraham Offers Isaac

The years passed, and Isaac grew to be a strong boy. Abraham was proud of his son and loved him very much. But one day God tested Abraham to see if he loved Isaac more than God. "Abraham," God said to him.

"Yes, here I am," Abraham answered.

"Take Isaac, whom you love so very much, and sacrifice him as a burnt offering on a mountain I will show you," God said. Abraham was hurt to hear this, but he would obey God no matter what He asked. So he took wood for the fire and left for the mountain with Isaac and two young servants.

On the third day Abraham and Isaac came to the place that God showed them. This was the land of Moriah. The two servants stayed with the donkey while Isaac carried the wood up the mountain. Abraham carried the knife and the flint to make the fire.

"Where is the lamb for the sacrifice?" Isaac asked.

"God will give it to us," Abraham answered. Abraham built an altar on the mountain and placed the wood upon it. Then he tied Isaac and laid him on the wood. But when Abraham lifted the knife, an Angel of the LORD called to him from heaven, "Put the knife down." God told Abraham, "I know now that you fear Me most of all." Then Abraham saw a ram caught by its horns in a bush. So he sacrificed the ram instead of Isaac.

God talked again to Abraham and told him how He would bless him with countless descendants.

Abraham went down the mountain and returned home again to Beersheba.

A Bride for Isaac

Abraham was worried about his son Isaac. So he talked with his oldest and most trusted servant. Perhaps that servant could help.

"You must not let Isaac marry one of the women around here," said Abraham. The Canaanite women who lived nearby did not know the God of Abraham and Isaac. Not one of them would be a good wife for him.

"Go to my homeland and find a wife among my relatives," said Abraham. He knew that his relatives would teach their children about God.

So the servant left with ten camels loaded with wonderful things. He went north where Abraham's relatives lived.

"O God," the servant prayed, "show me the right woman for Isaac." The servant decided to wait at a spring where the young women of the village came for water. He would ask some for a drink of water. The one who would offer to water his camels also would be the right one for Isaac. That was the way God would show him the woman He wanted.

While the servant was still praying, Rebekah came with a water jug on her shoulder. She was beautiful, and the servant wondered if this was the right one. So he asked her for a drink of water.

"Of course," she said. "And I will water your camels also."

The servant was happy as he watched Rebekah water all his camels. Surely God had helped this happen. Rebekah's family were happy to hear about Isaac and were glad that she could marry him. The servant must have been happy too. He knew that God had chosen this bride for Isaac.

Esau Sells His Birthright

Isaac and Rebekah were very happy together. But they had no children. Many years passed, then at last they had twin sons. The older son was named Esau, and the younger son was named Jacob.

As the boys grew up, hairy red-faced Esau became a hunter. Jacob was a quieter young man who liked to help around the home. Thus the father, Isaac, came to like Esau better, while the mother, Rebekah, came to like Jacob better.

One day Jacob was making a pot of lentil stew when Esau came home from hunting. "Give me some of your stew," Esau told Jacob.

"I'll trade you some stew for your birthright," said Jacob.

"When a person is starving, what good is a birthright?" said Esau. "It's a deal!"

"Promise me before God that you mean it," said Jacob.

So Esau promised before God that he was trading his birthright for the stew. A birthright in those days meant the older son got twice as much as any other child. He also became the leader of the family when the father died.

So Jacob gave Esau the stew with bread, and Esau ate it. Then he went on with his work as if he had done nothing unusual.

Many years later, Esau would be sorry that he had done this. But it would be too late then to change what had happened.

Isaac Refuses to Fight

Isaac and his family were shepherds, so they moved from place to place to find good pasture. Once they moved to the Gerar Valley where his father, Abraham, had lived. Abraham had dug wells there years before, but when he died, the Philistines filled the wells with dirt.

Now Isaac began to take the dirt from the wells so he could have water for his animals. Isaac and his men also dug a new well. It was especially good, with lots of water from a spring.

But the Philistines came and started a big argument. "This is our land and our well," they said. Isaac refused to fight, so he let them have the well and dug another.

The Philistines argued about that one too. Isaac again refused to fight and let them have the well. Then he and his men dug another one. This time the Philistines did not argue about it. "Now the Lord has made room for all of us," said Isaac.

Isaac moved on to Beersheba after that. One night God spoke to him. "I am with you and will bless you," God told Isaac. "I will give you many descendants and they will be a great nation." Isaac built an altar there and settled down to live there a while. He and his men also began to dig another well there at Beersheba.

Visitors came from Gerar to see them. King Abimelech of the Philistines was there with his advisor and his general.

"Why are you here?" Isaac asked. "Certainly you don't want to be friends."

"Yes, we do," they answered. "We can see that God is with you. So let's agree that we will not fight each other."

Isaac was pleased and so he made a great feast. It was a happy day, for shortly after that, Isaac's men came with the good news that they had found water in the well they were digging.

Jacob's Ladder

Jacob was a runaway. He had to run away from home. That's because he had tricked his father, Isaac, when Isaac was old and blind.

Isaac thought he was giving the family blessing to Jacob's twin brother Esau, Isaac's favorite son. But he gave it to Jacob instead. Jacob tricked him into doing this.

When Esau heard about this he was angry. He even said he would kill Jacob. That's why Jacob had to run away. But Jacob was a man now. With God's help, he could take care of himself.

Jacob traveled all day. In the evening, it was time to stop. After he ate, Jacob lay down, his head on a rock. It wasn't like his pillow back home. But it was all he had.

That night Jacob dreamed a strange dream. A long ladder that looked like a stairway appeared. It went all the way to heaven. In his dream Jacob saw angels walking up and down on the ladder. Suddenly the Lord appeared at the top of the ladder.

"I am the Lord, the God of Abraham and Isaac," the Lord said to Jacob. "I am giving this land to you and your children."

When Jacob woke up he was afraid. "God is here!" he said. "This must be the gate of heaven." So Jacob named that place Bethel, which meant "God's House."

That was a good name, don't you think?

Joseph's Coat of Many Colors

A father should not love one son more than another. That's called "playing favorites." That's what Jacob did. He loved Joseph more than any of his other 11 sons. The other sons knew this too, for Jacob did special things for Joseph.

The other brothers grew jealous of Joseph. So they began to behave like spoiled little boys, even though they were men.

When Joseph helped his brothers take care of the family sheep, he often came home and told his father about the bad things they did. These things were true, of course, but Joseph's brothers hated him even more for doing this.

One day Jacob gave Joseph a beautiful coat, or cloak, with many colors. This cloak showed that his father thought he was more important than any of the other brothers. The brothers hated Joseph even more when they saw the beautiful cloak.

Things grew worse when Joseph had two dreams and told his brothers.

In one dream he and his brothers were binding sheaves of grain in a field. Suddenly the brothers' sheaves bowed down to Joseph's sheaf. That meant that some day the brothers would bow down before Joseph.

In the other dream, the sun, moon, and eleven stars bowed down to Joseph. That meant that Joseph's father and the other brothers would bow down before him. You can imagine how much the brothers hated Joseph now. They began to plan how they could hurt him.

Joseph Is Sold as a Slave

Joseph's brothers were angry and jealous because their father liked Joseph more than them. Jacob had given Joseph a beautiful cloak that showed he was more important than his brothers.

Then Joseph had two dreams. These dreams showed that the brothers would bow down before Joseph some day. That's why they were jealous and angry.

"Let's kill Joseph," some of the brothers said. "We'll tell our father that a wild animal did it." But Reuben, the oldest son, did not like that. He tried to think of a way to help Joseph.

"No," he said. "Let's put Joseph into a pit instead." Reuben planned to come back later to rescue Joseph. Since Reuben was the oldest, the other brothers did what he said. They tore Joseph's cloak from him and threw him into a deep pit.

While Reuben was away, some traders came by, headed toward Egypt. "Let's sell Joseph," his brother Judah said. "Then we won't have to kill him."

So the brothers sold Joseph to the traders. The brothers were sure that he would become a slave in Egypt. He would have to work so hard that he would die before long.

When Reuben returned, he was angry. But what could he do? Joseph was gone. Joseph's brothers tore his cloak, put goat's blood on it, and took it to their father.

"Some animals have killed him," said Jacob. "I will cry for him as long as I live."

Joseph Becomes Governor of Egypt

Have you ever heard of men who sold their brother as a slave? That's what Joseph's brothers did. They sold him to some traders on their way to Egypt.

In Egypt, Joseph was sold to an officer named Potiphar. Some officers would have been cruel to Joseph and made him work under the hot sun all day. But Potiphar was kind to Joseph and let him take care of his house.

Before long, Potiphar saw how many good things were happening because of Joseph. So he put Joseph in charge of his entire household. Joseph did well. Potiphar was pleased. He liked Joseph.

Potiphar's wife liked Joseph also. She even fell in love with Joseph. One day Potiphar's wife asked Joseph to go to bed with her. But Joseph would not do it. He knew God would not like that. Potiphar would not like it either.

Potiphar's wife was angry at Joseph. She lied and said he had tried to hurt her. So Potiphar put Joseph into prison.

Many months went by. Then Pharaoh, king of Egypt, had some strange dreams. But no one could tell him what they meant. Then one of the king's officers remembered Joseph. Joseph had helped the officer understand his dream.

Pharaoh called for Joseph, and Joseph did tell him what his dreams meant. A famine was coming. Pharaoh needed a wise governor to prepare for it. "You will be that wise governor," Pharaoh said.

So in one day, Joseph the slave became the second most important man in Egypt. God was with him, wasn't He?

The Hebrews Become Slaves

When Joseph became governor of Egypt, the Egyptians had plenty of food to eat. But people in other countries did not. So Joseph brought his family to Egypt. He gave them a place to live, land for their herds, and plenty of food.

As time passed, Joseph and his brothers and his father all died. Their children had many children. And these children had many, many children. These people, who became known as Hebrews, filled the land of Goshen. That was the part of Egypt where they lived.

Pharaoh, king of Egypt, began to worry about the Hebrews. He was afraid there would soon be more Hebrews than Egyptians. "If war comes, they may join our enemy," he said. "We must find a way to stop them now."

Pharaoh forced the Hebrews to become slaves. He had cruel taskmasters tell them what to do. They built two cities called Pithom and Rameses.

But the Hebrews kept having more and more children. Being slaves did not keep them from having children.

Pharaoh ordered some Hebrew nurses to kill all Hebrew boys as soon as they were born. The girls could live. But the nurses did not obey Pharaoh. They knew God would not be pleased.

"Why haven't you obeyed me?" Pharaoh demanded. "Because the Hebrew women have their babies too fast," the nurses answered. "We don't get there in time."

The Hebrew people kept on having babies. At last Pharaoh had another plan. He ordered his soldiers to throw all Hebrew baby boys into the Nile River.

Moses Is Born

Two Hebrew slaves, Amram and Jochebed, had a new baby boy. They were afraid that Egyptian soldiers would find him and throw him into the river. Pharaoh, king of Egypt, had ordered his soldiers to kill all the Hebrew baby boys.

Jochebed hid the baby boy at home for three months. But it was getting harder to hide him. She knew someone would find him before long.

One day Jochebed made a little basket. She wove bulrushes together. She covered the outside with asphalt and pitch to keep water out. Then she put her baby boy in this basket and set it among the reeds at the edge of the Nile River.

Miriam, the baby's sister, hid by the river. As she watched, Pharaoh's daughter came there to bathe. Suddenly the princess saw the little basket and sent a servant girl to get it. When Pharaoh's daughter opened the basket, she saw the baby boy. He was crying, and she felt sorry for him.

"This must be a Hebrew baby," she said.

Miriam came quickly to talk with the princess. "Shall I find a Hebrew woman to take care of the baby for you?" she asked.

"Yes," said the princess.

Miriam ran home and brought her mother to see Pharaoh's daughter. "Take care of the child," she told Jochebed, "and I will pay you."

When the boy was old enough to leave his mother, Jochebed brought him to the princess. The boy became her son and lived in the palace with her. The princess named him Moses, which meant "drawn out" because she drew him out of the water.

The Burning Bush

Moses became the son of the princess. He grew up in the palace and was taught to be a prince. He had everything he wanted. But one day Moses got into trouble. He had to run away from Egypt to a land called Midian. He had to live there many years.

Moses became a shepherd in Midian. He married Jethro's daughter Zipporah and took care of Jethro's sheep.

One day Moses was watching the sheep in the desert near Horeb, the mountain of God. Suddenly the Angel of the LORD appeared to Moses in a flame of fire in a bush. Moses watched the bush burning, but it never burned up. When he went closer to see what was happening, God spoke to him.

"I want to deliver My people from their slavery in Egypt," God told Moses. "You will lead them to a good land. I will send you now to Pharaoh. Tell him that he must let these people go."

God showed Moses two signs. When Moses put his shepherd's rod on the ground, it became a serpent. When he picked it up, it became a rod again. That was one sign. When Moses put his hand into his cloak and took it out, he had leprosy. When he did this again, he was well. That was the other sign.

"I can't speak well," Moses complained.

"I will send your brother Aaron with you," God told Moses. "He is on his way here now to see you."

Moses had no more excuses. So he headed back home to tell Jethro what had happened.

God Sends Plagues to Egypt

God told Moses to go to Egypt and lead the Hebrew slaves to a new land. His brother Aaron would go with him and help him. When Moses and Aaron reached Egypt, they went to see Pharaoh, king of Egypt.

"Let My people go," Moses demanded.

"I will not," said Pharaoh. Then the king made the Hebrew slaves work hard to gather straw and then to make bricks without straw. The Hebrews still had to meet their quota.

Moses went back to Pharaoh. He told Aaron to throw down his rod, and it became a serpent. Surely the king would see this miracle and know that God sent Moses. Then Pharaoh would let the people go.

Pharaoh had his magicians do the same thing. But Aaron's serpent swallowed the others. Still Pharaoh would not let the Hebrew people go.

Moses and Aaron kept coming back to Pharaoh. Each time they did some miracle from God. One time God changed water into blood. He also sent frogs, lice, flies, boils, hail, and locusts. One of the worst plagues that God sent was darkness. It lasted three days. The Egyptians were so afraid. But Pharaoh still would not let the Hebrew people go.

At last God sent the worst plague. Every firstborn Egyptian died, even Pharaoh's firstborn.

At last Pharaoh let the Hebrew people go. That same night they left Egypt. They took their animals and families. They even took gold and silver and jewels from the Egyptians. At last the Hebrew people were free. They were no longer slaves in Egypt.

The Exodus

What a sight! There were thousands and thousands of Hebrews leaving Egypt. God had sent ten terrible plagues upon Egypt. Nine times Pharaoh stubbornly refused to let the Hebrews go. But when all the firstborn of Egypt died, Pharaoh told them to leave.

The Egyptian people wanted the Hebrews to leave, too. They gave them gold and silver and jewels. They were afraid they would all die.

The Hebrews left Egypt the same night the firstborn of Egypt died. There were thousands of men on foot, plus all the women and children. And there were flocks and herds, and wagons filled with their things.

"This is a day for you to remember," Moses told the people. "The Lord brought you from Egypt with great miracles. Each year at this time, you must remember this special day, of the LORD's Passover. When you do, be sure to tell your children why you are celebrating. Remember also when you come into the Promised Land that your firstborn belong to the Lord. And your firstborn animals belong to Him, too."

God Sends Pillars of Cloud and Fire

The Hebrew people left Egypt from Rameses and headed toward Succoth. Moses took the bones of Joseph with him, for his ancestors promised to do this.

From Succoth, the people moved on to Etham, at the edge of the great wilderness. But God did not take them on a direct route to the Promised Land from there. He knew they would be discouraged if they had to go through the land of the Philistines. The Philistines would be sure to fight them. Although the Hebrews had weapons, they were not ready to form an army and fight so soon.

God took the Hebrews through the Red Sea wilderness. As they traveled each day, God guided the people with a pillar of cloud. At night, God guided them with a pillar of fire. Even when they stopped, the pillar of cloud and the pillar of fire were there. It never left them, for God was always with them.

Crossing the Red Sea

"Tell the people to camp along the shore of the sea," God told Moses. "Pharaoh will think you are trapped there and will come after you. Then I will show him that I am the LORD."

Moses did what the Lord said and camped along the shore of the sea. Pharaoh heard about this. Suddenly he changed his mind about the Hebrews and wanted them back as his slaves. Pharaoh got into his chariot and led the best 600 chariots of his entire army after the Hebrews.

The Hebrews were terribly afraid when they saw the army coming. They began to complain to Moses. "You must not be afraid," Moses told the people. "Watch and you will see the wonderful way the Lord will rescue you."

The Angel of God moved the pillar of cloud between the Egyptian army and the Hebrews, so the Egyptians could not find them. That night it was dark on the Egyptian side of the cloud, but on the Hebrew side there was light.

While this was happening Moses stretched out his hand over the sea. All night a strong wind blew, and the Lord opened a path through the sea. The water moved aside like great walls, and the bottom of the sea became dry.

The Hebrews walked through the sea on the dry ground. When the Egyptians followed, the Lord caused their chariot wheels to fall off.

When the Hebrews were safe, the Lord told Moses to stretch out his hand again. The sea rushed back, and all the Egyptian army drowned.

The Hebrew people looked at this wonderful miracle and realized what the Lord had done for them. So they trusted the Lord and His helper Moses.

Food in the Wilderness

When God saved the Hebrew people from the Egyptian army, they sang a song. Moses' sister Miriam played a tambourine and sang. Other women followed her, dancing and singing to the Lord, praising Him for His help.

After that, Moses led the people into the Wilderness of Shur. After three days without water they came to Marah. But the water there was too bitter to drink. The people grumbled again and said things about Moses that they should not have said. "What shall we drink?" they complained.

Moses asked God to help. So God showed Moses a tree that would sweeten the water. When Moses threw the tree into the water it was good to drink.

When they arrived at the Wilderness of Sin, there was no food, and so the people complained again. "We had plenty of food in Egypt," they said. "We should have stayed there. We will starve here."

"I will send food," the Lord told Moses. So Moses and Aaron told the people what the Lord said.

That evening quails flew down and covered the camp. Now the people had meat to eat. In the morning there was dew on the ground and when it left the people saw thin white flakes in its place.

"This is the bread the Lord gives you," Moses told them. "Gather it the way He said." Some listened and gathered only enough for one day, as the Lord said. Others tried to gather more, but it rotted and smelled.

Moses was angry because they did not obey. The people called this bread *manna*. It was white and tasted like wafers made with honey.

69

Water from the Rock

When the Israelites left the Wilderness of Sin, they traveled from place to place as the LORD led them. One place was called Rephidim, where there was no water.

The people grew thirsty and quarreled with Moses. "Give us water!" they demanded.

"Why are you complaining to me?" Moses asked. "Why are you testing the Lord?"

But the people were thirsty, and so they kept on grumbling and complaining. "Why did you bring us out of Egypt so we would die of thirst here?" they said.

Moses prayed and asked the Lord what to do. "These people are ready to kill me," he said.

"Take some leaders with you," the Lord told Moses. "When you get to the rock at Horeb, hit it and water will come out."

Moses did what the Lord told him, and he hit the rock so the leaders could see. Then water came from the rock, as the Lord said it would.

Moses called this place Massah, which meant "testing." That was because the people tempted the Lord. He also called it Meribah, which meant "contention." That was because the people quarreled about the water.

The Ten Commandments

Moses led the people through the wilderness until they came to Mount Sinai. One day Moses went up into the mountain. The Lord spoke to him there and gave him ten special rules. These rules are so important that we still learn them today and try to do what they say. Here are God's ten important rules:

1. You must not worship any other god than Me.

2. You must not make any idol, or bow down and worship any idol.

3. You must not say My name in a foolish way, or curse with it.

4. You must keep the Sabbath Day holy. Work six days each week and rest on the Sabbath.

5. Honor your father and mother.

6. You must not murder.

7. You must not pretend that another person's husband or wife is your own.

8. You must not steal.

9. You must not lie about someone.

10. You must not covet something that belongs to another person.

When Moses came down from the mountain he told the people what God had said. Then there was thunder, lightning, the sound of the trumpet, and smoke on Mount Sinai. The people were afraid and begged Moses to speak to them for God. They were afraid they would die if God talked to them.

But Moses told the people not to be afraid of God. They should obey Him and keep His commandments. Then they would have nothing to fear.

The Golden Calf

While Moses was on Mount Sinai, getting the Ten Commandments from the Lord, the people waited below. But it took a long time for the Lord to give Moses all the rules and plans. While Moses was there, the Lord gave him all the plans to make the tabernacle and the things that would go in it.

"We don't know what has happened to Moses," the people said to Aaron, Moses' brother. "Make gods to lead us."

Aaron asked the people for their gold earrings. He melted the gold and made a golden calf with it. "This is our god," some people said. The next day the people had a big party and danced around the golden calf.

"Go down from Mount Sinai," the Lord told Moses. "Your people have made an idol like a calf. They are bowing before it. Let Me punish them."

But Moses begged the Lord. "Please don't turn against the people and hurt them," he said. "If You do, the Egyptians will say You brought them here to kill them." So the Lord did not hurt the people.

Moses went down from Mount Sinai with the two tablets of stone on which the Ten Commandments were written. When Moses went into the camp where the people were dancing before the golden calf, he was angry. Moses threw down the two tablets, and they broke into pieces. Moses burned the golden calf and ground it into powder. He scattered it on water and made the people drink it.

Moses was angry at Aaron for making the golden calf. But Aaron made an excuse. "I just put the gold into the fire and out came this calf," he said.

The Lord sent a plague because of the the golden calf. That was His punishment for what Aaron and the people had done.

The Tabernacle

"**B**ring special offerings to the Lord," Moses told the people. "Bring what you want to give." Moses would use these gifts to make the tabernacle, the tent of God. God would meet with Moses in the tabernacle and tell him what the people should do.

The work began, with Bezalel and Oholiab guiding the other craftsmen. They both had great skill in this kind of work. Each day people kept bringing more gifts for the tabernacle.

One day the workers told Moses, "We have more than enough things to finish the work." So Moses told the people to stop giving.

The tabernacle became a beautiful tent, with sheets of linen and draperies of goats' hair and rams' skins for the roof. The frames for the side were acacia wood, covered with pure gold and set in silver bases. A linen drape covered the front.

Inside the tent was the ark, a wooden chest covered with gold. On the lid were two cherubim, like angels, facing each other. Inside were the stones on which the Ten Commandments were written.

Special bread was placed on a wooden table covered with gold. A gold lampstand had seven lamps on it. There was also a wooden incense burner, covered with gold.

In the courtyard there was a large bronze bowl where priests washed before they did their work for God. And there was also a big altar where priests burned offerings to the Lord.

As long as the people lived in the wilderness, this tent was God's house. They moved it with them each time they went to a new place. When they came to the Promised Land, they put it in one place and left it there for many years.

Twelve Spies

"**S**end spies into the land of Canaan," the Lord said. Moses sent twelve spies into Canaan to see what it was like.

The spies went into Canaan for forty days. When they came back through the Valley of Eshcol, they cut a branch with a large cluster of grapes and brought it with them.

"This land is a good land," the spies said to Moses and the people. "There are wonderful things growing there. But the people are strong. Some are giants. And their cities have tall walls."

Ten spies warned the people not to go into Canaan. "We felt like grasshoppers beside these people," they said.

But two spies, Joshua and Caleb, told the people, "Don't be afraid of these people, for the Lord will help us."

That night the people of Israel cried and said some terrible things about Moses and Aaron. "Let's choose someone to take us back to Egypt," they said. The people even talked about stoning Joshua and Caleb.

Moses and Aaron were sad. But the Lord told Moses what to say to the people. "Not one of you twenty years or older will go into this land. You must stay in the wilderness for forty years. Your children will go in, but you will not."

So the people had to stay in the wilderness for forty years. Most of them died there because they had not trusted the Lord. They never saw the land God had promised.

The Bronze Serpent

The people of Israel lived in the wilderness for forty years. Sometimes they moved from one place to another. The Lord would not let them go into the Promised Land because they had not trusted Him to help them.

At one of the campsites along the way, somewhere between Mount Hor and the Red Sea, the people began to grumble again. They wanted to go through Edom but the king of Edom would not let them. Now they had to go many miles out of the way.

The grumbling people began to say things against God and Moses. They grumbled about the food and water. And they grumbled about the wilderness.

Then the Lord sent poisonous snakes into the camp. Many people died because of the snakes.

"We have sinned!" they said to Moses. "We should not have said what we did about you and the Lord. Please ask the Lord to take the snakes away."

Moses prayed and the Lord told him what to do. "Make a bronze snake and put it on a pole," the Lord told Moses. "Whoever has been bitten by a snake may look at this bronze snake and live."

That is the way it happened. Anyone who had been bitten by a poisonous snake could look at the bronze snake and would not die.

Balaam's Donkey

King Balak of Moab was afraid of the Israelites. They had already defeated his neighbors, the Amorites. Now they were camped near his land.

The Moabites asked another neighbor, the Midianites, to help. But they were still not strong enough to fight the people of Israel. So they sent messengers to a prophet named Balaam, asking him to come and curse the people of Israel. They thought this would hurt the Israelites.

"Stay here tonight," Balaam told the messengers. "I will ask the Lord what to do." When he did, the Lord told him not to go with the men.

King Balak sent more and more important messengers. The Lord told Balaam to go if the men came to call him. But Balaam did not wait to be called. When the Lord saw Balaam ride on his donkey with the men, He was angry. Then the Angel of the Lord stood in the road in front of the donkey. The donkey saw the angel but Balaam did not. So the donkey ran off the road into a field.

Balaam struck his donkey to turn her back onto the road. But this time the donkey squeezed close to a wall to stay away from the angel. Balaam's foot was hurt, so Balaam struck the donkey again.

Now the angel moved ahead to a place where the donkey could not pass. This time the donkey lay down on the road. Balaam struck her again. Suddenly the donkey began to talk. Then the Lord let Balaam see what the donkey had seen.

"Go with these men, but say only what I tell you," the angel said.

Balaam went with the men. Then he told King Balak, "I will say only what the Lord tells me to say." And he did. Balaam would not curse the people of Israel, for the Lord told him not to do it.

Jericho's Walls Fall Down

The people of Jericho were afraid. They had heard stories about the Israelites. They had heard how God had led the Israelites from Egypt with many miracles. They had heard how God had taken care of them for 40 years in the wilderness.

Now the Israelites were ready to conquer the Promised Land. Jericho was the first city. That's why the people of Jericho were afraid.

God told the Israelites what to do. And so one day the Israelites marched from their camp to Jericho. They quietly marched around the city. But they did not fight. Then they went back to camp. The next day they did the same thing.

They did this for six days. Each day the people of Jericho prepared to fight. But each day the Israelites marched back to camp. The people of Jericho became more afraid each day.

On the seventh day the Israelites marched around Jericho seven times. Suddenly they stopped. The priests blew their trumpets. The Israelites shouted. You have never heard such a shout.

The walls of Jericho began to shake and fall to the ground. Now the people of Jericho were terrified. They began to run. But there was no place to run. The Israelites rushed into Jericho and captured it. Then they burned the city.

The battle for Jericho was over. God had helped the Israelites win with the blast of trumpets and a shout.

Gideon's Three Hundred

Gideon was a brave leader. But he had a problem. He had 32,000 soldiers. And the Midianite army he had to fight had 120,000 soldiers.

Gideon talked with God about this problem. "You don't need more soldiers. You have too many now," God told Gideon. "If you win, your soldiers will think they did it. They must know that I will win this battle for you. Send some of them home."

So Gideon called his men together. "Anyone who is afraid may go home," he said. Only 10,000 stayed.

"You still have too many soldiers," God told Gideon. "Take them down to the river to drink water. I will tell you which ones to keep."

Some men got down on their hands and knees to drink. "Send them home," God told Gideon. Now there were only 300 soldiers left with Gideon. They were the ones who lapped water from their hands.

One night Gideon gave each of these soldiers a trumpet, a torch, and a clay pitcher. The soldiers covered their torches with the pitchers and went to a hill above the enemy camp.

At Gideon's signal the soldiers blew the trumpets and broke the pitchers.

When the Midianites saw this, they were afraid and ran away. God helped all of this happen. So God helped Gideon defeat an army of 120,000 with only 300 brave soldiers.

Now you know God helped Gideon win. So did Gideon and his soldiers.

The Story of Ruth

"I want to go home," said Naomi. Years before, Naomi and her husband Elimelech left Israel during a famine. There was no food in Israel, so they went to live in Moab. But Elimelech died there in Moab.

Their two sons, Mahlon and Chilion, married two Moabite women, Ruth and Orpah. Then Mahlon and Chilion died. Now Naomi was alone in a foreign land with her two foreign daughters-in-law. That's why she said, "I want to go home."

"We will go with you," Ruth and Orpah said.

"No, you must stay here in your own land," Naomi told them. Orpah stayed in Moab. But Ruth would not stay.

"I will go with you wherever you go," she said. That showed how much Ruth loved Naomi.

So Ruth went with Naomi to Israel. But what would these two women eat? Someone had to work in the grain fields to pick up grain that the harvesters left. There was no other food at this time. Naomi was too old to work in the fields, and so Ruth worked to earn enough for both of them.

One day Boaz, the owner of the fields, fell in love with Ruth. He saw what a wonderful woman she was. Ruth learned what a wonderful man he was too. Ruth and Boaz were married.

Naomi was so happy that these two wonderful people had found each other. So she lived happily ever after with them.

Samuel Is Born

In the days when the Judges ruled Israel, there was a man named Elkanah who had two wives. In those days some men married more than one wife.

Peninnah, one of Elkanah's wives, had children. That was a great honor in Israel at that time. Peninnah made fun of the other wife, Hannah, who had no children. Poor Hannah was so sad and ashamed that she often cried.

Each year Elkanah went to Shiloh with his family to worship at the tabernacle, God's house. Each year Peninnah made fun of Hannah.

After dinner one evening Hannah went to the tabernacle and began to pray to the Lord. "Give me a son, and I will give him back to You," Hannah prayed.

Eli the priest, the man in charge of the tabernacle, saw her. He saw her moving her lips but didn't hear her praying, so he thought she was drunk. "How long will you be drunk?" he demanded. "Stop doing that!"

"But I haven't been drinking," said Hannah. "I am praying that God will give me something special."

"Then may He do it," said Eli.

Hannah was happy to hear Eli say that. Now she was sure God would give her a son. Some time later Hannah did have a baby boy. She named him Samuel, which meant "heard by God" because as she said, "I asked God to give me this boy."

Of course Hannah was very happy with her new son. And she remembered her promise to give him to God.

Samuel Serves at the Tabernacle

Hannah was so happy with her new son. For a long time she could not have children. Then she had prayed, asking God to give her a son. "If You do, I will give him back to You, to serve You all his life," Hannah promised.

Now Hannah had her son. And she remembered her promise to God. The year after Samuel was born, Hannah's husband, Elkanah, went back to Shiloh to worship at the tabernacle, God's house. His other wife, Peninnah, went too, with her children. But Hannah did not go.

"Let's wait until Samuel is weaned," she told her husband. "Then I will take him to God's house and leave him there with Eli to serve God."

"We will do what you think is best," Elkanah told her. "Let God's will be done."

So Hannah stayed home at Ramah until Samuel was weaned. Then she and Elkanah took him to Shiloh, to leave him with Eli to serve at God's house. Samuel was still just a little boy.

"Do you remember who I am?" Hannah asked Eli. "I prayed here at God's house that He would give me a son. He answered my prayer, and gave me Samuel. Now I am giving him to the Lord to serve Him the rest of his life."

Hannah left Samuel at the tabernacle to serve God. Then Hannah prayed a beautiful prayer. "I am filled with joy because God answered my prayer," Hannah prayed. "No one is as holy as God. He feeds the starving people and gives children to those who cannot have them."

After that, Hannah returned home to Ramah with her family. But the boy Samuel stayed there at the tabernacle with Eli to help Eli do God's work.

God Speaks to Samuel

When Samuel was still a little boy, his mother, Hannah, gave him to the Lord. She brought him to the tabernacle, God's house. Samuel became God's helper, and a helper for old Eli, the priest, the man in charge of the tabernacle.

God did not speak often to people in those days, so what happened one night to the boy Samuel was quite unusual. This is the way it happened. Eli, whose eyes were getting dim, had gone to bed. So had Samuel, who slept in the holy inner room of the tabernacle where the Ark of the Covenant was kept. Suddenly God called to Samuel.

"Samuel! Samuel!" He said. Samuel thought Eli had called, so he ran to see what he wanted.

"Go back to bed," Eli said. "I did not call you." This happened three times.

"If God calls you again, say that you are listening," Eli told Samuel.

When Samuel went back to bed, God did call again. "I'm listening," Samuel said to God. Then God told Samuel what He was going to do to Eli and his sons.

"I will punish them all," He said. "I have warned them about this."

Samuel stayed in bed all night. In the morning he opened the tabernacle doors as he always did. He was afraid to tell Eli what God had said. "You must tell me all that God said to you," Eli told Samuel. So Samuel told Eli what God had said. "God must do what He thinks is best," said Eli.

As the boy Samuel grew to be a man, people could see that God was with him. So they listened to Samuel. They knew that he would be God's prophet. God did give Samuel more messages. And Samuel told the people what God said.

The Ark Is Captured

In a war between Israel and the Philistines, the Israelites were losing. So they retreated to talk. "Let's carry the ark of the covenant into battle," they decided. The ark was at the tabernacle at Shiloh.

So it was brought to the army camp at Ebenezer. Hophni and Phinehas, sons of Eli the priest, came with it and helped take it into battle. The Israelite soldiers shouted so loud when they saw the ark that they frightened the Philistines.

"The Israelite God has come to their camp," the Philistines said. "Fight harder than you have ever fought!"

The Philistines did fight harder. And they won. They even killed 30,000 Israelites and captured the ark.

One man escaped and ran to tell the old priest Eli the bad news. He was ninety-eight years old, blind, and fat. When he heard that the ark was captured and his sons killed in battle, Eli fell backward, broke his neck, and died.

The Philistines took the ark back to the temple of their god Dagon in Ashdod. The next morning they found Dagon's statue fallen down, with his face bowing to the ark. The next night the same thing happened, but this time Dagon's head and hands were broken off. Then a plague broke out in Ashdod.

The Philistines knew they were in trouble because of the ark. They decided to send the ark to Gath. When they did, the people there got the plague. They then sent it to Ekron, but the people there cried out against it.

At last the mayors of the five Philistine cities got together and urged the people to send the ark back to Israel. They were afraid of what might happen next.

The Return of the Ark

For seven months the Philistines kept the ark of the covenant in their land. They had captured it from the Israelites, but it had brought them much trouble. Each city where the ark was taken had a bad plague.

At last the Philistine people were too afraid to keep the ark any longer. They called for their priests and sorcerers. "How should we return the ark to Israel?" they asked. "What gift should we send with it?"

"Send five golden tumors, like those we got in the plague," they answered. "And send five golden rats, like those that brought the plague. Put the ark in a new cart and hitch it to two cows that have new calves. Put their calves in a barn and these golden things next to the ark in the cart. Let the cows go. If they go to the Israelite city Beth Shemesh, you will know all this trouble came because we took the ark. If they stay here, you will know the plague came by accident."

The people did exactly as the priests and sorcerers said. The cows headed straight for Beth Shemesh in Israel, lowing as they went. The five mayors of the Philistine cities went as far as Israel.

The people of Beth Shemesh were harvesting wheat when they looked up and saw the ark coming. They were very happy. As the cart came into the field of a man named Joshua, it stopped near a big stone. The people broke the cart into pieces, built a fire, and sacrificed the cows as an offering to the Lord.

The five Philistine mayors watched a while and then returned to Ekron. They had sent the golden tumors and golden rats from their five cities—Ashdod, Gaza, Ashkelon, Gath, and Ekron.

Saul Is Made King

Samuel became a great judge, a ruler over Israel. He was a good one, too, for he went from place to place, helping people know what God wanted them to do.

Samuel grew old and made his sons judges in his place. His sons, Joel and Abijah, ruled at Beersheba. But they were dishonest men and took bribes. At last the leaders of Israel had enough of this. They went to Samuel and demanded, "We want a king like the other nations around us." Samuel was upset and talked to the Lord about this.

"Warn them how a king will reign over them," the Lord said. But the people still wanted a king. Then the Lord told Samuel that Saul, the son of a wealthy man named Kish, would be king. Samuel took some oil and poured it on Saul's head. That was called anointing. It showed Saul and others that Saul would be king.

Saul was a tall man. Most people just reached his shoulders. When Samuel brought the people together and told them Saul would be their king, the people shouted, "Long live the king." Samuel told the people what they must do. He wrote in a book what the king should do and put it in a special place before the Lord.

Not all of the people were happy with their new king. Some troublemakers said, "How can this man save us?" They did not even bring their new king a present, as the others did. But Saul said nothing about it.

Saul Sacrifices Wrongly

During his first year as king, Saul led his people to a great victory over some enemies. The people were sure now that he would be a strong king.

Saul kept about 3,000 of his troops together to defend Israel against the Philistines, a greater enemy than the one he had conquered. He set up camp with 2,000 at Michmash, while his son Jonathan took 1,000 and attacked some Philistines at Geba, destroying all of them. Saul called for the entire army to gather now, for the Philistines were angry.

But the Philistines gathered a much larger army. They had 3,000 with chariots, 6,000 on horses, and more than they could count on foot.

Now the Israelite soldiers became so afraid that they ran away. They hid in caves, among rocks, and even in tombs and cisterns. Some crossed the Jordan River to Gad and Gilead.

But Saul stayed with some trembling troops at Gilgal. Seven days earlier Samuel had told Saul to wait for him to come and make a sacrifice to the Lord. Samuel said he would be there in seven days.

Now Saul saw his men running away and decided not to wait for Samuel. He would make the sacrifice himself, even though he should not do that. Just as Saul was finishing, Samuel arrived.

"What have you done?" he asked Saul. "God told you what to do, and you have not obeyed Him. He will not let you or your sons keep on ruling as king. He will choose another who will obey Him." Then Samuel left.

Jonathan's Bravery

King Saul had only 600 men left. The Philistines had thousands, with horses chariots and swords. Saul's men did not even have swords.

One day Saul's son Jonathan headed toward the Philistine camp with the young man who carried his armor. They had to climb up the steep wall of a ravine to get there.

"If the Philistines tell us to stay where we are, that will be God's way of telling us not to fight," said Jonathan. "But if they tell us to come up, that will be God's way of telling us to go and fight."

When the Philistines saw Jonathan, they told him to come up. So, Jonathan and his armorbearer climbed up the steep wall to the Philistine army camp. Suddenly the Philistines began to fight each other. Saul and his 600 men joined the battle, along with the men who had run away from Saul's army.

The Philistines began running from Saul's men. Then Saul made a foolish vow. "A curse on anyone who eats before evening," he said.

Jonathan did not hear what Saul said. So when they went through a forest, he dipped a stick into a honeycomb and ate some honey. When evening came Saul asked the Lord if they should keep going after the Philistines. But the Lord would not answer.

"We must find out what sin was done today," Saul said. "Whoever has sinned must die." Saul found out that Jonathan had eaten some honey. "You must die for this," he said. But the soldiers of Israel would not let that happen.

"Jonathan saved Israel today," they said. "He must not die." So they would not let Saul execute Jonathan.

Samuel Anoints David

Saul was a good military man, leading his army to some great victories. But he was not the kind of king God wanted. Saul did not always obey God. Of course even a king needs to obey God. Samuel was sorry to see this happen.

"You have felt sorry long enough," God told Samuel one day. "Go to Bethlehem. I have chosen a son of Jesse to be the next king."

"Saul will kill me if he hears what I am doing," said Samuel.

"Take a heifer and make an offering there," God said. "When you do, I will show you which son is to be king. Then you can anoint him" Samuel did exactly what God said.

This must be the one, Samuel thought when he saw Jesse's first son, Eliab.

"No he isn't," God said. "You must not judge by appearance. I don't look at others that way. I look at their heart."

Jesse brought seven of his sons to Samuel. "God has not chosen any of these to be the next king," Samuel told Jesse. "Do you have any other sons?"

"The youngest is watching the sheep," said Jesse.

"Bring him here now," Samuel said. "We will not sit down until he has come." Jesse brought David, a good-looking young man with the well-tanned face of an outdoorsman.

"This is the one I have chosen," God told Samuel.

So Samuel poured oil on David's head while his brothers watched. Then God's Spirit came upon David.

David and Goliath

The Philistine soldiers gathered between Suchoh and Azekah for a great battle. Saul gathered his Israelite army at the Valley of Elah. The Philistines were on one side of the valley and the Israelites on the other side.

One day a Philistine giant named Goliath came out into the valley. He was over nine feet tall, with a bronze helmet, a 125 pound armored suit, and bronze leg coverings. He carried a bronze javelin with a 16 pound iron head. His armor bearer carried a large shield for him.

Goliath shouted to the Israelites. "Send a man to fight me. If your soldier kills me, we will be your servants. If I kill him, you will serve us." Saul and his soldiers were afraid. They heard Goliath shout this every day for 40 days, twice each day.

One day Jesse sent his son David to the army camp with food for his brothers—Eliab, Abinadab, and Shammah, who served in Saul's army. David heard Goliath shouting and it made him angry. "I'll go fight this Philistine!" said David.

"All right, do it," said King Saul. "May God be with you." At first, Saul put his armor on David. But David could not walk. So he took five smooth stones from the brook and put them in his shepherd's bag. Then with his shepherd's staff and sling, he went to fight Goliath.

Goliath was angry that one so young came to fight this way. But David said, "I come to fight in the name of the Lord. He will conquer you."

As Goliath rushed toward him, David whipped a stone at Goliath with his sling. The stone sank into the giant's forehead, and he fell dead to the ground.

David grabbed Goliath's sword and cut off his head. When the Philistine soldiers saw that they ran. The Israelites chased them and won a great battle.

The Friendship of David and Jonathan

Jonathan, son of King Saul, had watched as David went out to fight the Philistine giant Goliath. No other man would do this, and David was not even a soldier in Saul's army.

When David was brought to Saul, Jonathan admired him greatly. The two became close friends and developed a strong bond of love that day. Jonathan swore that he would be like a brother to David. To show that he really meant this, he gave David his robe, his sword, his bow, and his belt.

King Saul decided to keep David at the palace instead of letting him go home to Bethlehem. He made David his army commander. The soldiers were delighted that David would lead them.

But something strange happened the day David killed Goliath. On the way home some women came out singing and dancing with tambourines and musical instruments. They sang about David's killing ten thousands and Saul's killing only thousands. This made Saul jealous, for it gave more honor to David than to Saul.

"Now *what* more can he have but the kingdom." Saul grumbled. So he began to watch David carefully.

Saul Tries to Kill David

King Saul was jealous. After David killed Goliath, some women sang songs about David's killing tens of thousands while Saul killed only thousands. Saul wondered if the people would try to make David king instead of him.

The next day Saul was distressed. David played the harp for him, as he often did, to soothe him. Saul held his spear while David did this. Then suddenly Saul threw the spear at David, hoping to pin him to the wall and kill him. David jumped aside. This same thing happened another time. Saul became so jealous that he demoted David to captain. But this only made David more popular. David behaved wisely in all he did, and Saul became even more jealous.

Saul offered his older daughter Merab to David in marriage. But then Saul had her marry a man named Adriel instead. Then another of Saul's daughters, Michal, fell in love with David. Saul offered to let David marry her. "All you need to do is kill 100 Philistines," Saul told David. So David and his men killed 200. Then David married Michal.

When David became more popular than ever, Saul tried to get Jonathan and some others to kill him. But they wouldn't.

"David has always tried to help you," Jonathan told Saul. "Why should you try to kill him now?" For a while Saul did not try to kill David. But one day when Saul was listening to David play the harp, he threw his spear at him again and almost killed him. Then Saul ordered his men to kill David when he left his house in the morning. But Michal learned of this plan, and helped David escape during the night.

Jonathan Warns David

"Why does your father want to kill me?" David asked his friend Jonathan.

"But he doesn't," said Jonathan. He did not realize how much King Saul, his father, wanted to kill David.

"Your father would not tell you that he wants to kill me," said David. "He knows we are good friends."

"But what can I do?" Jonathan asked.

"Tomorrow starts the three-day feast of the New Moon," said David. "I won't be there. If Saul is angry, tell me and we will know he wants to kill me."

So Jonathan and David planned a signal. The next day David would hide by a pile of rocks. Jonathan would shoot three arrows nearby. Jonathan would send a boy after the arrows. If he told the boy that the arrows were on this side of him, David would know all was well. But if he said the arrows were beyond him, David would know Saul wanted to kill him.

On the third day of the feast Saul asked Jonathan about David. Jonathan gave an excuse that he and David had planned. Saul was so angry that he tried to kill Jonathan. Then Jonathan knew for sure that Saul wanted to kill David.

The next morning Jonathan shot the three arrows. When the boy ran for them, Jonathan called out, "the arrow is beyond you." That was the signal that Saul really did want to kill David.

When Jonathan sent the boy back to town with his bow and arrows, David came from his hiding place. The two friends shook hands and cried.

"Let's remember what we have promised," Jonathan told David. They were such good friends they had promised to be kind to each other and to each other's children as long as they lived. So David left and Jonathan went back to town.

Abigail Shares Her Food

After Samuel died, Saul kept on hunting David, trying to kill him. He was jealous, afraid that David would become king instead of him. David had to keep moving around.

Once he came to the Wilderness of Paran. There a wealthy man named Nabal owned a sheep ranch near Carmel. As long as David and his men camped nearby, the shepherds and their flocks were safe.

One day, this man Nabal was at the ranch shearing sheep. He was a rude man with poor manners, while his wife Abigail was beautiful and intelligent.

David depended on men like this to feed him and his men as they wandered around, trying to keep away from Saul. So he sent 10 men to ask Nabal for food.

But Nabal was rude and insulted David and his men. So David left camp with 400 men to attack Nabal. While this was happening, one of Nabal's servants told Abigail what Nabal had done.

Abigail quickly gathered 200 loaves of bread, 2 jars of wine, 5 butchered sheep, 1 bushel of roasted grain, 100 clusters of raisins, and 200 fig cakes. She took these things on donkeys to David's camp.

David was still grumbling about Nabal when Abigail rode up with these things. She got off her donkey, bowed before David, and gave him the food.

"Praise God for sending you," David told her. "If you hadn't come, not one of Nabal's men would have been alive in the morning."

When Abigail told Nabal about this the next morning, he was so angry that he had a stroke. After lying there paralyzed for 10 days, he died. When David heard that, he sent for Abigail and married her.

David Spares Saul

David had to keep moving around from place to place, hiding from King Saul. The king wanted to kill him because he was jealous and afraid David might become king.

Once when David was at the hill of Hachilah, the men from the Wilderness of Ziph nearby told Saul where he was. Saul took 3,000 of his best soldiers and camped near there. David's men knew all of this, for they had spies watching.

One night David and Abishai went down to Saul's camp. Saul and his general, Abner, were sleeping inside a circle of sleeping soldiers. David and Abishai slipped through these, until they came to Saul. "Let me kill Saul," said Abishai.

"No," said David. "God chose him to be king. God must take his life some day." David took Saul's spear and jug of water. Then he and Abishai slipped from the camp without anyone's knowing it.

When they had climbed safely on a mountain ridge nearby, David shouted. "Wake up, Abner!" he called. "Why haven't you guarded your king? Where is the spear and jug?"

Saul heard David and knew who it was. "Is that you, my son?" he called.

"Yes," David answered. "But why are you after me? What have I done wrong?"

"I have been wrong to chase you," Saul admitted. "Come home, and I will not harm you. You have saved my life today."

David gave Saul's spear to one of Saul's young men. Then David slipped away, and Saul went back home.

But David did not go home, for he did not trust Saul now. He knew that Saul might still try to kill him.

Saul Dies in Battle

One day the Israelites and Philistines fought on Mount Gilboa. Many Israelites were killed. The rest ran away. Even King Saul and his sons tried to run away. But the Philistines caught them. They killed Saul's sons—Jonathan, Abinidab, and Malchishua.

The Philistine archers went after King Saul. They wounded him with their arrows.

"Kill me!" Saul told his armorbearer. "If you don't, they will torture me."

The armorbearer was afraid to kill his king. So Saul fell on his own sword and died. The armorbearer also fell on his sword and died.

The Israelites on the other side of the valley heard what had happened. They were afraid and ran away. Then the Philistines came and lived in their towns.

The next day the Philistines went to the battlefield to take things from the dead Israelites. When they found Saul and his sons, they cut off Saul's head. They took his armor, and sent word throughout the land that King Saul was dead.

The Philistines hung Saul's armor in the temple of the Ashtoreths. They hung his body on the wall of Beth Shan.

But brave Israelite warriors from Jabesh Gilead marched all night. They took the bodies of Saul and his sons back home and burned them there. Later they buried their bones under the tamarisk tree in town. Then they fasted for seven days.

David Becomes King

After Saul died, David asked the Lord if he should go home to Judah. When the Lord said yes, David asked where he should go.

"To Hebron," the Lord told David.

David moved to Hebron, not far from his boyhood home at Bethlehem. He took with him his two wives, Ahinoam and Abigail. Some of David's friends also came with their families.

One day the leaders of Judah came to Hebron and made David their king. They anointed him, pouring oil on his head. This was the way leaders showed that the Lord was making someone king.

David was pleased that the people of Jabesh Gilead had buried Saul. He sent them a message. "The Lord will bless you, and I will be kind to you because you did this," David told them. "Now that Saul is dead, the leaders of Judah have made me their king."

Abner, commander of Saul's army, had taken Saul's son Ishbosheth to Mahanaim. The people there made Ishbosheth king over the rest of Israel. He was forty and ruled for two years. David ruled over Judah for seven and one half years.

David Captures Jerusalem

One day some men killed Saul's son Ishbosheth. Then the leaders of Israel came to David at Hebron. "You are our king now," they told David. They anointed him with olive oil.

David was 30 at this time. He ruled for 40 years. He was king of Judah for seven and one half years. Then he was king of all Israel for 33 years.

After David became king of Israel, he wanted a new capital. Jerusalem was a strong-walled city. It was also called Jebus at that time. It would make a fine capital.

But the Jebusites already lived there. They were enemies. They thought David could not conquer it. "Even our blind and crippled men could keep you from taking this city," they mocked.

David sent his men up through the water tunnel. They captured the fortress of Zion. So this became David's new home and capital. He named it the City of David and built more around the fortress. He started his building program on the east side where the land was filled in.

The Lord was with David, and so he became stronger each day. Hiram, king of Tyre, gave David cedar logs, carpenters, and stone masons. David built a beautiful palace. He knew that the Lord was blessing him and his people.

When David moved to Jerusalem he married more wives and had more children. His children born in Jerusalem were Shammua, Shobab, Nathan, Solomon, Ibhar, Elishua, Nepheg, Japhia, Elishama, Eliada, and Eliphelet. Do you know anyone with any of these names?

The Ark Is Moved

"Let's bring the ark of God to Jerusalem," David told his officers. They thought it was a good idea. So David ordered 30,000 soldiers to go with him to Kirjath Jearim. The ark was in a house there.

The ark was a beautiful golden chest that Moses had made in the wilderness. Inside were two tablets of stone with the Ten Commandments on them.

This day the ark was placed on a new cart, guided by Uzzah and Ahio. The ark had been in their father's home for many years. There was singing and dancing and music as the ark was taken to Jerusalem.

Suddenly one of the oxen pulling the cart stumbled. Uzzah grabbed the ark to hold it steady. But the Lord was angry at the way he did it. Uzzah dropped to the ground. He was dead.

David was afraid now and took the ark to the home of Obed-Edom nearby. There it stayed for three months.

One day David decided to try again. This time he had it carried the way God said. What a great time this was, with music and dancing.

At last the ark was placed in the tent that David had made for it. Then David and his people gave offerings to God.

David showed his thankfulness by giving each person there a loaf of bread, a piece of meat, and a cake of raisins. Imagine taking home special gifts from the king!

David Is Kind to Mephibosheth

"Is any of King Saul's family still alive?" David asked one day. "I would like to help him." Saul's son Jonathan had been David's special friend, even though Saul often tried to kill David.

Someone remembered Ziba, a servant of Saul's family. He would know. So some people brought Ziba to King David. "One of Jonathan's sons is still living," Ziba told the king. "He is crippled."

Before long Mephibosheth was there, standing in front of David. But he didn't stand long. He bowed down before the king. He must have been shaking. Would David kill him because Saul had tried to kill David?

"Don't be afraid," David told Mephibosheth. "Your father and I were good friends. So I will give your grandfather's land to you. You may eat with me from now on."

Mephibosheth bowed before the king again. What a kind man David was!

From that day on, Mephibosheth lived in Jerusalem. He ate with the king, and the king treated him like a son.

David and Bathsheba

Late one afternoon David went to the roof of his palace. As he walked around, he saw a beautiful woman. She was taking a bath at her house below.

"Who is she?" David asked.

"Bathsheba, Uriah's wife," someone told him.

David sent for Bathsheba and went to bed with her. Later Bathsheba learned that she and David were going to have a baby. She sent someone to tell the king.

David wanted Uriah to think this was his baby. He brought Uriah home from a battle at Rabbah. But Uriah would not go to bed with his wife. He thought it would be wrong to do this when his friends were fighting a battle.

David sent Uriah back to his army commander with a note. "Put Uriah in the front lines to be killed," David said.

After Uriah died, David married Bathsheba. The Lord was not pleased. He sent the prophet Nathan to talk to David.

Nathan told King David a story about a rich man who stole a poor man's pet lamb. David was angry. "That man should die!" he shouted.

"You are that man!" Nathan said. "God will punish you for killing Uriah and stealing his wife. The child that you and Bathsheba have will die."

Things happened the way Nathan said. When the boy was born he was sick for a week. Then he died. Later David and Bathsheba had another son and named him Solomon. He would become the next king of Israel.

Absalom Rebels Against David

David's handsome son Absalom decided that he wanted to be king. He would rebel against his father and become king of Israel. But first he must win many of Israel's leaders to him.

This is the way he did it. Absalom got a chariot and horses and rode to the city gate each day. People came with their complaints, and Absalom listened to them. "If I were judge, I would do more for you," he would say. Many began to wish he was king instead of David. Before long many leaders were ready to make him king.

One day Absalom went with some leaders to Hebron. He had them make him king. David and his trusted men ran away when they heard this. David would not fight his son. When David was gone, Absalom moved into his palace in Jerusalem. He made plans to kill his father so no one would keep him from being king.

Absalom had two advisors. Ahithophel was loyal to him. But Hushai was secretly loyal to King David. Hushai gave advice that seemed good but would hurt Absalom.

One day Hushai advised Absalom to lead an army against David. Absalom listened to Hushai. He did not know that Hushai had sent word to David to prepare his soldiers for this battle. Absalom's men were defeated, and Absalom was killed. The plot to kill David had failed.

Water from the Wells of Bethlehem

Before he became king, David was hiding from King Saul in the cave of Adullam. In those days the Philistines camped in the Valley of Rephaim. Some were in Bethlehem, David's hometown.

During the harvest time, three of Israel's bravest soldiers came to see David. "Oh, how I want a drink of water from the well of Bethlehem," David said. He was talking about the well by the town gate.

The three brave soldiers went to Bethlehem and fought the Philistines. When they brought water for David, he would not drink it. Instead, he poured it out as an offering to the Lord.

"I can't drink this water," David said. "These men risked their lives to get it. This would be like drinking their blood."

David Buys a Threshing Floor

"Count all the men who could be soldiers," David told his army commander Joab. "Why do you want to do that?" Joab asked. He knew that David should not be proud. He should not depend on the number of men he had. He should depend on the Lord.

But David wanted to do this anyway, so Joab and his men counted all the men who could become soldiers.

"There are 800,000 in Israel and 500,000 in Judah," Joab said.

After David did this, his conscience bothered him. "I have sinned, forgive me!" he told the Lord.

The Lord sent Gad the prophet to see David. David could choose how the Lord would punish him.

"Which one will it be?" Gad asked David.

"Will you have seven years of famine, three months of running from your enemies, or three days of a bad disease in the land?"

"We can't be punished by men," David answered. "Let the Lord punish us Himself with the disease. He is merciful and will know when to stop." So 70,000 people died from disease. On the third day the angel of death was at the threshing floor of Araunah. The angel was ready to destroy Jerusalem.

"Stop!" the Lord said. "That's enough." Then the Lord told David to build an altar at this place to honor Him.

David bought the threshing floor and some oxen from Araunah for 50 pieces of silver. There he built an altar to the Lord and gave offerings upon it. Later David's son Solomon would build a great temple at this place.

David Plans the Temple

King David wanted to build a temple for the Lord. It would be at the threshing floor which he bought from Araunah. But the Lord would not let him do it. David had been a man of war and had killed too many people. "Solomon, your son, will build My temple," the Lord told David.

While David was still king, he made plans for the temple. He gathered much of the building material. He had almost 4,000 tons of gold and 40,000 tons of silver. He also had jewels, bronze, iron, wood, and stones. David found workmen to build the temple and take care of it.

David called the leaders of his people together. He told them that Solomon would build the temple, as the Lord commanded.

"Serve the Lord," David told his son Solomon. "Build His house. If you are with the Lord, He will be with you. If you turn against Him, He will forsake you."

Before all the people, David praised the Lord. "Praise the Lord," the people answered.

Solomon was made king, and Zadok became the priest. The whole nation respected Solomon and promised to be loyal to him.

Solomon's Wisdom

Solomon ruled wisely, and the Lord was with him. One day he took officials and leaders with him to Gibeon. There he gave a thousand burnt offerings on the altar at Gibeon.

That night the Lord appeared to Solomon in a dream and promised to give whatever he asked. "Give me an understanding heart to judge my people," said Solomon.

The Lord was pleased with Solomon's choice. "You will have wisdom," He promised. "Since you did not ask for money and honor, I will give those to you, too."

Later Solomon showed how wise he was. Two women brought a baby to him. "It's my baby," said the first woman. "We live together. The other night this woman rolled over on her baby and smothered it. She put her dead baby beside me and my baby beside her."

"No, it's my baby," said the second woman. Then the women began to argue.

"Bring a sword," said Solomon. When someone brought a sword, Solomon ordered the baby cut in two. "Give half to each woman," he said.

"No!" said the first woman. "Don't do that! Let her have the baby."

"Cut the baby in two," said the other woman.

"Give the baby to the first woman," said Solomon. "She is the real mother."

The people had great respect for Solomon when they heard about this. They knew the Lord had made him wise.

Solomon Builds the Temple

King Solomon sent messengers to King Hiram of Tyre. "You were my father's friend," he said. "You sold cedar logs for his palace. Please work with me as I build the temple."

Hiram was glad to sell cedar logs to Solomon. He also sent Huram, a wise master craftsman. Huram helped Solomon build the temple.

Solomon built the temple on Mount Moriah. King David had bought Ornan's threshing floor there. The temple was 90 feet long and 30 feet wide, with two large bronze columns at the entrance.

Solomon built a large bronze altar and a large bronze tank where the priests could wash. He built ten basins to wash animal meat for offerings. He made golden lampstands, golden bowls, and many beautiful pieces of equipment to use for the offerings. At last the ark of the covenant, the golden box with the Ten Commandments inside, was put in the Most Holy Place.

When the temple was finished, Solomon prayed before the people who gathered there. "Listen to our prayers and bless us," Solomon prayed.

Fire came from heaven and burned the meat on the altar. In a dazzling light, the glory of the Lord filled the temple. When the people saw this, they fell down and worshiped the Lord. After a great feast, the people went home, happy that the Lord was blessing them.

Solomon Is Rich and Famous

Almost everyone heard about King Solomon. He was rich and famous. And he was very wise. When the queen of Sheba heard, she came to Jerusalem. She wanted to meet this wise man.

The queen brought many attendants. She had camels loaded with gold, spices, and jewels.

The queen asked Solomon many difficult questions. He answered each one wisely. The queen saw that he was wise. She saw that he had a wonderful palace, food, and staff.

This woman was rich too. She brought gifts for Solomon. There were four and a half tons of gold and the best spices he had ever received. Solomon also gave her many fine gifts.

Solomon got riches from many other places. Merchants paid him gold and silver for taxes. Kings and governors paid him tribute. And he made profit from his trade with other nations.

Solomon had so much gold that he thought silver was common. Every three years Solomon's fleet of ships came with more riches. He was richer and wiser than any other king, and people wanted to listen to him.

King Solomon had many horses and chariots. He even began a business, buying and selling them. Each important person who visited Solomon brought more gifts. This went on year after year. No wonder he became so rich and famous!

Solomon Turns from God

King Solomon did not need to fight wars as his father, David, had done. He chose to make peace with his neighbors another way.

Solomon married seven hundred princesses. What king would fight a man married to his daughter? That's why neighboring kings kept peace with Solomon.

But these princesses brought strange gods into Israel. There was Ashtoreth and Milcom and Chemosh. Solomon even let his wives build altars to these gods just outside Jerusalem. By the time Solomon was old, his wives had gotten him to do evil by worshiping these other gods.

The Lord talked with Solomon twice and told him not to worship these gods, but Solomon did it anyway. So the Lord was angry at Solomon. He told him, "I will take your kingdom from you and your son when you die. I will give it to one of your officials."

One day the prophet Ahijah talked to Jeroboam. He was Solomon's official in charge of forced labor. Ahijah tore his new robe and gave ten pieces to Jeroboam. "The Lord says He will take the kingdom from Solomon," said Ahijah. "When Solomon is dead, He will give you ten tribes. But He will let Solomon's son keep one tribe with Jerusalem."

Solomon heard about this and tried to kill Jeroboam. But Jeroboam ran away to Egypt. He stayed until Solomon died.

After Solomon ruled forty years, he died. He was buried in the City of David in Jerusalem.

The Kingdom Divides

When Solomon died, his son Rehoboam went to Shechem. He wanted the ten northern tribes of Israel to make him king.

Jeroboam heard of Solomon's death and came home from Egypt. He and other leaders of Israel went to see Rehoboam. "Treat us better than your father Solomon did, and we will be loyal to you," they said. "Come back in three days and I will give you an answer," said Rehoboam.

Rehoboam talked with his older advisors. "Treat these people kindly," they said. "If you do, they will serve you."

Then Rehoboam talked to his younger advisors. "Tell them you will not be as kind as your father Solomon," said the younger men. So that is what Rehoboam said.

The leaders of the ten tribes of Israel rebelled against Rehoboam. They killed Adoram, Rehoboam's man in charge of forced labor. Rehoboam got into his chariot and escaped to Jerusalem.

Then the leaders of Israel made Jeroboam king of their ten tribes. Rehoboam was king over the tribe of Judah, where Jerusalem was located.

Now there were two kingdoms: the Northern Kingdom, the Southern Kingdom.

149

Ravens Feed Elijah

Think of the worst people you ever met. King Ahab and Queen Jezebel were much worse. They were very wicked people. That's why they did not like Elijah, God's helper.

God helped Elijah do many wonderful things. They were called miracles. But God would not help the wicked king and queen.

Of course they never asked God to help them. They believed in other gods, such as idols made of wood or stone or gold. They did not believe in Elijah's God, even though they had seen His miracles.

One day God sent Elijah to King Ahab. He wanted to show Ahab that there really is a God in heaven and that God helped Elijah do miracles.

"There will be no dew or rain in Israel for years until I say so," Elijah told the king. That's what God told Elijah to say. The king didn't believe him, of course. How could a man stop the rain? A man can't stop the rain, but God can. He would stop the rain. That would be a miracle.

God also told Elijah to hide by the Brook Cherith where he would have water to drink. God would do a second miracle there. He would have ravens bring Elijah's food to him. So each morning ravens brought Elijah's breakfast. Each evening they brought his dinner.

God did two miracles for Elijah: He stopped the rain, and He sent ravens to feed Elijah. Do you think Elijah trusted God to do what He said?

A New Room for Elisha

There was once a kind woman who lived with her husband in a little town called Shunem. Whenever Elisha, God's prophet, came to town, the womam invited him to eat with them.

One day this kind woman decided to do something special for Elisha. "Let's make a room for Elisha upstairs," she said to her husband. He thought that was a good idea. So they did it.

"Let's put some furniture in this room," the woman said.

So she and her husband put a bed, a table, a chair, and a lamp in the room. Elisha would have a lovely place to stay whenever he came to Shunem.

The next time Elisha came to town he went to see this kind woman and her husband. Of course he was not expecting anything special.

"We have a surprise for you," the woman told Elisha.

You can imagine how surprised Elisha was when he saw the lovely room.

"You may stay here whenever you come to Shunem," she said.

Do you suppose Elisha thanked the woman and her husband for this lovely room? Do you suppose he thanked God for this kind woman and her husband?

Naaman the Leper Is Healed

Long ago, General Naaman had captured a little slave girl in a battle in Israel. She helped take care of his wife. "Why are you crying?" the little slave girl asked.

"Because Naaman has leprosy," the wife answered. Leprosy was a terrible disease. Most people with leprosy had to live alone, away from their families.

The little girl was sad. She knew that Naaman and his wife loved her. And she had learned to love them.

"He should go to see Elisha," said the little girl. "Elisha can help him get well." Then she told Naaman's wife about the wonderful miracles that Elisha had done. The woman then told Naaman and begged him to go to Elisha. But Naaman did not know where to find Elisha. So he first went to see the king of Israel. The king was angry. He thought Naaman was trying to trick him. But Elisha knew about Naaman's visit. So he told the king to send Naaman to him.

When Naaman reached Elisha's house, he was surprised. Elisha did not even come out to meet him. Instead, he sent a servant. "Go to the Jordan River," the servant said. "Wash in it seven times."

Naaman was angry. He started home. But his servants begged him to do what Elisha had said. Naaman went to the Jordan River. He washed seven times. Suddenly he was healed. So Naaman praised God and said he would worship Him as long as he lived.

The Story of Jonah

"Go to Nineveh," God told Jonah. "Preach to the people there."

Nineveh! Jonah thought. *That is a very wicked city. Those people will kill me.*

Jonah decided to run away from God. Of course, you know that nobody can do that. Jonah must have known that too. But he tried.

Jonah went on a ship headed far from Nineveh. He was tired, and so he lay down and fell asleep.

But God sent a great storm. The wind blew. The waves of the sea pounded on the ship.

"We'll die!" the sailors cried out.

"Pray to your God!" the captain shouted to Jonah. But Jonah was running away from God. How could he pray to God when he was running away from Him?

At last Jonah knew why God had sent the storm. God had found him.

"Throw me into the sea," Jonah told the sailors. "Then the storm will stop."

When the sailors threw Jonah into the sea, the storm stopped. But Jonah didn't drown. God sent a big fish to swallow him. For three days, Jonah lived in that big fish. Then the fish spit Jonah out on dry land.

Jonah then went to Nineveh. He preached to the people there. And he probably never tried to run away from God again.

Daniel Refuses to Eat the King's Food

It was a sad day in Israel. Babylonian soldiers broke through the walls of Jerusalem. They killed many people. They captured others, such as Daniel and his three friends. Then the soldiers took these captives many miles away to Babylon.

One day an officer named Ashpenaz talked with Daniel and his three friends. "Good news," he said. "We will teach you how to be the king's helpers. You will go to our best schools. You will eat the food and wine that the king eats."

Daniel and his friends were given new names. Daniel became Belteshazzar. Hananiah became Shadrach. Mishael became Meshach. And Azariah became Abed-Nego.

Daniel and his friends were glad that they could have good jobs. That was better than being slaves. But they did not want to eat the king's food and wine. God would not be pleased if they did.

"Let us eat plain food," Daniel asked. At first Ashpenaz and his helper did not want to do this. They were afraid Daniel and his friends would not grow strong. Then the king would punish Ashpenaz and his helper.

"Let us try plain food for 10 days," said Daniel. So the officers let them try it for 10 days and saw that Daniel and his friends grew strong. The officers let them keep on eating the plain food. Daniel and his friends became the king's strongest and wisest helpers. That's because God was with them.

The Fiery Furnace

"All the people must worship me," said King Nebuchadnezzar. "Then they will know how important I am." The king had some men make a golden statue of himself. It was 90 feet high and 9 feet wide. He sent orders to all the important people of the land to come to the statue.

"When the musicians play you must bow down before the statue," the king's officers said. "If you don't you will be thrown into a fiery furnace."

Suddenly the music played. Everyone bowed down before the statue except Shadrach, Meshach, and Abed-Nego. The king was angry when he heard that.

"Bow down or I'll have you thrown into a fiery furnace," he commanded.

"We can't do that," the three friends answered. "We can bow to our God only."

The king was angrier now than before. "Make the furnace seven times hotter," he commanded.

Then some of the king's men shoved Shadrach, Meshach, and Abed-Nego into the furnace. But they did not die. They walked around in the furnace.

Then the king saw a fourth person in the furnace. "He looks like the Son of God," said the king.

Then the king ordered the three friends to come out. When they did, he could see they were not burned at all. "God sent His Angel to help these men," the king said. "Anyone who says a bad word about their God will be torn apart." So people honored God for the miracle He had done.

The Handwriting on the Wall

King Belshazzar had a party. He invited a thousand friends and officials of the land. He had food and wine, dancing and games. It was a big party that lasted a long time

Before long the people began to be bored. The king did not want that. So he decided to do something different. He would use the beautiful gold and silver cups he had captured from God's house, the temple.

"We will drink our wine from these sacred cups," the king said. Soon the cups were brought to the party. Servants poured wine and guests drank.

"What fun!" they thought. The king and his people began to praise the gods of Babylon. They began to laugh at God. Suddenly the king jumped to his feet. "Look!" he cried out. "What's that?"

A giant hand was writing on the wall. "Send wise men," said the king. "I must know what the writing says." But the king's wise men did not know.

"Send for Daniel," said the queen. "He will know."

Daniel did know. God told the king what the writing meant. "Your kingdom will end soon," said Daniel. "God will give it to other people."

At that moment, soldiers were coming through the city gates. By morning, King Belshazzar was dead. The big party was over. Others ruled the land now. The people who made fun of God must have begged Him for His help.

Daniel in the Lions' Den

King Darius liked Daniel. He had made Daniel and two other men governors. Now he planned to put Daniel over the other two men. He thought Daniel was the wisest man in the land.

The other two men did not like that. They were jealous. They wanted to be in charge. "Let's trap Daniel," they said. "Let's turn the king against him." But how could they do this? Daniel was a good man. He did not do bad things.

One of the men had an idea. "Daniel prays to his God three times each day," he said. "Let's make a law against praying and have the king sign it." The king was not thinking of Daniel when he signed it.

Before long the two men hurried to the king. "Daniel has broken your law," they said.

"He must be thrown into the den of hungry lions."

Now the king knew that he had been tricked. He was sad. He did not want to put Daniel in the den of hungry lions. But what could he do? He must keep the law.

So Daniel was thrown into the den of hungry lions. But the king could not sleep that night. He was worried. In the morning the king hurried to the lions' den. "Did your God take care of you?" the king called to Daniel.

"Yes," Daniel answered. "He sent His angel to shut the lions' mouths."

Then the king ordered the two bad men thrown into the lions' den. "I will make a new law," said the king. "Everyone must worship Daniel's God." Aren't you glad Daniel trusted God to help him?

The Story of Queen Esther

Esther was made queen. Of all the women in the land, the king had chosen her. Esther had an uncle named Mordecai. He had raised Esther as a child. He was sad to see Esther go to live in the great palace, but he knew God had something special planned for her.

One day the king, whose name was Ahasuerus, promoted Haman to a high position. Haman did not like Mordecai, however, because Mordecai would not bow down to him. All the other people bowed to Haman, but Mordecai would bow down only to God. That made Haman very mad.

So Haman thought of a plan to get rid of Mordecai. Haman knew that Mordecai was a Jew. And he knew that the Jews worshiped only God. So Haman tricked the king into signing a law that said that people could only worship the king. Those who worshiped anyone else would be killed. And sure enough, the Jews refused to worship the king.

So Haman went to the king and told him that the new law required that all the Jews in the land be killed. But Haman didn't know that Esther was Jewish too.

When Esther found out about Haman's plan, she invited Haman and the king to a special dinner. At the dinner Esther explained that she would soon die because she, too, was Jewish.

When the king heard this he got so mad that he ordered Haman hung on a gallows. So Esther saved her people.

John's Birth Announced

Zacharias and Elizabeth, his wife, were godly people, for they tried to obey God and His laws. But they were sad, for they were old and had no children.

One day Zacharias went to work as usual. He served as a priest. That week he had special duty in God's house, the temple. It was his job to go into a small holy room and burn incense to God.

While Zacharias did that, a crowd stood outside praying, as they usually did when a priest burned incense.

As Zacharias burned the incense an angel suddenly appeared and stood near the incense altar. Zacharias was surprised and afraid.

"Don't be afraid," the angel said to Zacharias. "I have come with special news. You and Elizabeth will have a baby boy, just as you have prayed. You will name him John.

He will be a great man for God."

"That is impossible," Zacharias argued. "My wife and I are too old to have a baby."

"I am Gabriel," the angel answered. "I have come from God with this message. But because you did not believe me, you will not speak until your son is born."

The angel left and Zacharias went out where the crowd was waiting. When the people saw that he could not speak, they realized that something special must have happened to him inside God's house.

When Zacharias finished his work at God's house, he went home to Elizabeth. They realized that the angel was right. They were going to have a baby!

Elizabeth was so happy about this. "God is so kind!" she said. "He is letting me have a child."

Jesus' Birth Announced

Mary was confused and frightened when she saw the angel Gabriel appear before her. "Good news for you," the angel said to her. "God is with you."

Of course Mary was not sure what to say. So she listened as the angel kept on speaking.

"Don't be afraid, Mary. God has something special planned for you. You will have a baby boy and will name Him Jesus. He will be great, the Son of God. He will be a king forever."

"But I have never been married," Mary argued. "How can I have a baby?" Mary was engaged to Joseph, one of King David's descendants. But they had not lived together yet.

"The Holy Spirit will come to you, and God's power will be upon you," the angel answered. "This baby will be God's Son." Then the angel told Mary about her cousin Elizabeth. "Six months ago Elizabeth found that she would have a baby," the angel said. "Every promise God makes will come true."

"I am God's servant," Mary said. "I will do whatever He wants. Let everything you said happen."

Then the angel departed.

Mary Visits Elizabeth

When Mary heard that her cousin Elizabeth was going to have a baby, she went down to see her. It was a happy time when they met, so happy that Elizabeth's baby jumped inside her.

"God has blessed you more than all other women," Elizabeth told Mary. "Your baby will receive God's greatest praise. Here you are, the mother of God's Son, visiting me. You have believed in God, so that is why He is doing this special thing for you."

"How I praise God," Mary answered. "How I rejoice in God my Savior. He saw me, a lowly servant, and has done something so wonderful that people for generations will call me blessed. God has done great things for me."

Mary stayed there with Elizabeth for about three months, and then she went home. Mary and her cousin Elizabeth had many wonderful things to think about. Each was waiting for a special baby to be born. Each baby was sent by God.

John the Baptist Is Born

The happy day came when Elizabeth had a baby boy. She was too old to have a baby, as you remember. But God worked a miracle so that Elizabeth and Zacharias could have this child.

All the friends and neighbors were happy when they heard this good news. It was quite a time of celebration when they all came for the circumcision ceremony. This was a special party when a baby boy was eight days old.

Everyone was sure that the baby would be named after his father. But Elizabeth said, "No, he must be named John."

"But no one in your family has that name," the people said. So they made gestures to Zacharias to ask what he thought. Zacharias pointed to a writing tablet. Then he wrote on it, "His name is John." As soon as he did that, he could talk again. So he began praising God.

The neighbors and friends were quite surprised at all this. Before long the news spread throughout the Judean hills.

People who heard about this wondered what would become of the child. It was clear that God had done something special with this boy.

Then God's Spirit came upon Zacharias, the boy's father, and he began to say wonderful things. "Praise God, for He is about to send us a Savior, as He promised long ago," said Zacharias. "And you, my son, will prepare the way for this Savior. You will help people know how to find salvation by having their sins forgiven."

So John grew up as a godly young man. But he chose to live in the wilderness until he became a minister for God.

Jesus Is Born

The Roman Emperor Caesar Augustus, ruled over much of the world at the time of these stories. He decided to take a census of all the people of his empire, so he gave his people orders to do this. That was about the same time when Quirinius was governor of Syria.

The census required everyone to go back to the place where their ancestors had lived. There people would register by families. Joseph was a member of the family that had come from King David. So he had to go to Bethlehem in Judea, where King David had lived as a boy.

So Joseph took Mary, who was almost ready to have her child, and made his way to Bethlehem. When they arrived, there was no room in the inn. So they had to stay in the stable with animals. That night, Mary's baby was born. She wrapped Him in long strips of cloth, and laid Him in a manger, where the animals ate.

Eight days later, at the circumcision ceremony, the boy would be named Jesus. That was what the angel had told Mary that God wanted. Of course Mary wanted to obey God.

Angels Appear to the Shepherds

One wonderful night, Jesus was born in Bethlehem. Not far away, in some fields outside town, shepherds watched their flocks of sheep. Suddenly an angel appeared to the shepherds. A bright light shined upon them. It was a special light from God. Of course the shepherds were surprised and frightened. But the angel tried to comfort them.

"Don't be afraid," the angel said. "I have wonderful news. It is the most wonderful news that anyone has ever heard. But this news is for all people everywhere. The Savior, God's Son, has been born tonight in Bethlehem. You may see Him there, wrapped in strips of cloth, lying in a manger."

A great choir of angels appeared in the night sky, and began praising God. "Glory to God!" the great angel choir sang. "Glory to God in the highest. Peace to all who please Him here on earth."

The shepherds had never heard such a wonderful choir. They had never heard such a wonderful song. What a night that was on the hills outside Bethlehem!

Shepherds Worship Jesus

When the great choir of angels finished singing, it suddenly disappeared.

The night sky was empty again except for the stars. The hills were quiet again except for a soft "baa" from a sheep here and there.

The shepherds stared at one another for a while. Had they really seen the angels? Had they really heard the choir singing? Had they heard the angel tell about the Savior, God's Son? Suddenly the shepherds knew what a wonderful thing they had heard. The Savior was born tonight, in Bethlehem!

"Let's go now to see Him!" the shepherds said to one another. "Let's see this Baby the Lord has told us about." The shepherds hurried to Bethlehem and found the stable where Mary and Joseph were staying.

How excited they were to see Baby Jesus, lying in the manger. This news was too good to keep. The shepherds went everywhere, telling the good news about the Savior who was born. People listened carefully, for this was good news that everyone had waited to hear.

Mary didn't say much about these things. But she was so happy and her heart was filled, like a chest full of treasure. Many times after that she thought about this wonderful night.

At last the shepherds went back to their sheep. They praised God often for the angels who had come to see them. And they praised God that they could see the Savior, the Baby Jesus.

Simeon and Anna Honor Jesus

When Jesus was eight days old, His parents circumcised Him, just as all good Hebrew parents did on the eighth day. There was a party, or ceremony. Mary and Joseph named Him Jesus, as the angel had told Mary long before He was born.

Some time after that, Mary and Joseph went to the temple, God's house, for another ceremony. Like other Hebrew mothers, Mary had to be purified, following the birth of her child. She had to give an offering of two turtledoves or two pigeons, for that was what the law said she should do. Since Jesus was Mary's first son, she also had to give Him to God.

While Mary and Joseph were there in God's house, an old man named Simeon saw them. The Holy Spirit had shown him that he would not die until he had seen the Savior. When he saw Jesus, he knew the Baby was the Savior he had waited to see. Simeon took Baby Jesus into his arms and praised God.

Mary and Joseph listened to all this and wondered. What did all this mean?

Simeon spoke to Mary next. "Some day you will be deeply hurt, for this Boy will be rejected by many of His own people. But He will also bring great joy to many others."

While Simeon was still talking, an old woman named Anna came along. She was a woman of God who lived there in the temple. When Anna saw Jesus, she began thanking God for Him. She knew that He was God's Son, the Savior. She began telling others that the Savior had come at last.

Mary and Joseph knew for certain then that their Boy was God's Son, the Savior. They must have thanked God many times that He had come at last.

Wise Men See a Star

When Jesus was born in Bethlehem, some wise men lived in a faraway land to the east. One night they saw a bright star they had never seen before. They knew this star was special, for it told them that a great King had been born.

The wise men set out at once to find this new King. They followed the star until it led them to the land of Israel. The wise men began asking people in Jerusalem about this new King. "Where is the new King of the Jews?" they asked. "We have seen His star in the East. We have come to worship Him."

King Herod was disturbed when he heard what these men were asking. He was the king. He did not want any other king to come and take his kingdom from him. People began whispering things about this King all over Jerusalem. So Herod called for the Jewish religious leaders.

"Do the prophets tell where this King will be born?" he asked.

"Yes, they do," the leaders answered. "The Prophet Micah wrote that a new Ruler would be born in Bethlehem."

When Herod heard that, he sent a message for the wise men to come to see him. "When did you first see the star?" he asked them. When they told him, Herod said, "Go and search for the Child in Bethlehem. When you find Him, come back here and let me know. Then I may go and worship Him, too."

Herod actually was plotting to kill this new King. He would not let another king take his kingdom from him.

The wise men did not know about Herod's plans. They were happy now that they had learned where this new King had been born. They would leave for Bethlehem immediately to find the new King.

Wise Men Visit Jesus

When the wise men left King Herod, they headed toward Bethlehem. There they would find the great King, the Savior. That's what the Jewish religious leaders had read in Micah, the prophet.

On the way, the special star they had seen appeared to them again. It led them to Bethlehem and stood over the house where Jesus lived with Mary and Joseph. When the wise men went into the house, they saw little Jesus at last. Then they knelt down before Him and worshiped Him.

These men had brought special gifts with them, which they gave to little Jesus now. There was gold, frankincense, and myrrh. Gold was used for money at that time. Frankincense and myrrh were expensive resins. Sometimes they were used in God's house when people worshiped Him there. That was a wonderful day for those wise men. They must have had a hundred questions to ask Mary and Joseph.

That night God warned the wise men in a dream. They must not go back to King Herod. They must go home some other way, because Herod wanted to kill young Jesus. The wise men did what God told them. They went home without telling Herod what they had learned.

Mary and Joseph thought often about this visit from the wise men. They knew by this time that Jesus was God's Son, the Savior and great King. But they had never expected a visit like this!

The Flight to Egypt

When the wise men left, Mary and Joseph looked again at the wonderful gifts the wise men had brought. There was gold, frankincense, and myrrh. They had never seen such beautiful gifts before.

That night an angel visited Joseph in a dream. "Get up!" the angel urged. "You must leave now for Egypt. Take Jesus and Mary and go! Hurry! King Herod plans to kill Jesus, so you must stay in Egypt until I tell you to leave." Joseph got up immediately. That same night he left for Egypt with Mary and Jesus. There they stayed until they heard again from the angel.

Before long, King Herod realized that the wise men were not coming back to see him and he was angry. He had made plans to kill little Jesus. But how could he kill Jesus when he did not know which child He was? The wise men had told Herod that they had seen the star almost two years ago. Herod knew only that Jesus was a boy somewhere in Bethlehem and that He was under two years old. "Kill them all!" Herod screamed. "Kill every boy in Bethlehem under two years old! Kill every boy around Bethlehem, too!"

Many years before, the prophet Jeremiah said this would happen. "There will be screams and crying around this region," he wrote. "Women will cry for their children and nobody can comfort them, for their children will be dead."

The mothers of Bethlehem did cry and scream for their dead boys. Wicked King Herod made many families hurt and cry. But he did not kill little Jesus. God's angel had taken care of Him and kept Him safe.

The Return to Nazareth

Mary and Joseph must have wondered each day how long they would have to stay in Egypt. An angel of God had told Joseph to take Mary and Jesus there. The angel had said they must stay in Egypt until he told them to leave. So the days and months passed.

Then one night an angel appeared to Joseph again in a dream. "Get up and take Jesus and His mother back to Israel," the angel said. "King Herod is dead."

Joseph left with Mary and Jesus. But on the way, he heard that Herod's son, Archelaus, was the new king. Would he be as bad as his father? Would he also want to kill little Jesus?

What should he do? That night, God told Joseph not to go back to Bethlehem. So Joseph took Mary and Jesus to Nazareth, in Galilee, instead. This was the town where Joseph and Mary had lived before Jesus was born. Some prophets had written about this many years before. They said that Jesus would be called a Nazarene, a man who lived at Nazareth.

Mary and Joseph were home at last. What a lot of things had happened since they left! But now they could raise the boy Jesus in their hometown. Now they could see Him grow up where they had lived so many years.

Jesus and the Carpenter's Shop

At last Mary and Joseph were home in Nazareth. This had been their hometown before Jesus was born. But they had left to go to Bethlehem to visit. The Roman emperor, who ruled the land, said they had to put their names on a census list there. And while they were there, Jesus was born. But they couldn't even stay at Bethlehem. An angel told them to take Jesus to Egypt. There they lived until the angel said they could come home.

Now that they were home, Joseph set up his carpenter's shop again. Each boy in Israel learned to do some special kind of work, usually learned from their father. Carpentry was the work that Joseph had learned when he grew up. That was the work he did as a man.

Now Joseph would teach Jesus how to be a carpenter. The boy Jesus made many things from wood. He hammered and sawed. He cut and polished. He made chairs and tables. He made bowls and wagon wheels.

Joseph was glad that he could teach the boy Jesus to be a carpenter. And Jesus was glad that He could work with wood, just as Joseph did.

Jesus and the Teachers

Each year the boy Jesus went to Jerusalem with His family for the great Passover feast. It was like a big party, with everyone in the country invited. When Jesus was twelve, He went with His family again to the Passover. As usual, they ate and talked with friends and relatives.

When at last the feast was over, crowds of people gathered in caravans and headed back to their homes. Jesus' family headed back toward Nazareth. There were aunts and uncles and cousins and many other family members in this caravan. It wasn't unusual for a boy to be walking with an uncle or aunt or cousin. So it wasn't until that evening, when the caravan stopped for the night to rest, that Mary and Joseph realized that Jesus was not there. They looked everywhere—with every aunt and uncle and cousin they could find. But Jesus was not with them.

Mary and Joseph headed back to Jerusalem. They looked everywhere for Jesus. At last, three days later, they found Him. There He was, sitting in the temple, God's house, talking with the teachers. Jesus was asking some very tough questions and giving some very good answers.

"Why have You done this to us?" Mary asked the boy Jesus. "Your father and I have been worried. We have looked for You everywhere."

"Didn't you know I must be about My Father's business?" Jesus asked. Jesus went home to Nazareth with Joseph and Mary. He was an obedient boy, as you would expect.

Mary thought often about what had happened. She must have wondered what it all meant. So Jesus grew up there in Nazareth. He became a wise young Man. God loved Him, and so did those who knew Him.

Jesus Is Tempted

The Holy Spirit led Jesus into the barren wilderness. Jesus had decided not to eat while He was in the wilderness. Forty days without food! Before long, Jesus would get very hungry and weak.

Satan knew this would be a good time to tempt Jesus. He would try to get Jesus to do something wrong, to sin.

So Satan came to Jesus and said to Him, "Why don't You turn these stones into bread? A miracle like that will show that You really are the Son of God.

Jesus knew that Satan was trying to trick Him. There was nothing wrong with eating bread. And turning stones into bread wasn't a sin. But Jesus had given up His God-given power so that He could be tempted like we are. It would have been the wrong time to do a miracle. If He had done a miracle, Jesus wouldn't have known what it was like to be tempted and say no.

"I won't do that," Jesus said. "The Scriptures say bread can't feed a person's soul. Only God's Word can."

Satan tried one more time. He took Jesus to the top of a tall mountain. "Look," Satan said. "I'll give You all the nations of the world if You will just bow down and worship me."

"Go away from here," Jesus replied. "The Scriptures say that we are to worship and obey only God."

So Satan tried again. He took Jesus to the roof of the temple and said, "Jump off! The angels will catch You." But Jesus would not listen to him.

Then Satan went away, and angels came to care for Jesus. Satan knew he could never get Jesus to do wrong.

The Woman at the Well

It was a hot day. When it was time for lunch, Jesus and His disciples stopped by an old well. The disciples went into the nearby town to buy some food. But Jesus stayed by the well. Soon a woman came to the well to draw water.

Jesus asked her, "May I have a drink of water?" The woman was surprised that Jesus talked to her. Jesus was a Jew, and the woman was a Samaritan. Most Samaritans and Jews did not like each other. But Jesus loves all people. He wants everyone to know about God.

So Jesus said to her, "If you knew who I really was, you would ask Me for water. And I would give you living water."

"But how would You get this water?" the woman asked. "You don't even have a rope or a bucket."

"If you drink the water from this well," Jesus said, "you will get thirsty again. But if you drink the water I give you, you will never be thirsty again."

"Please give me some of that water!" the woman replied. "Then I won't have to walk out to this well each day." Jesus knew the woman did not understand what He was saying.

So He began telling her things she had done long ago, things no ordinary person would know. "You must be a prophet," she said.

"I am the Messiah," Jesus replied.

The woman believed Jesus. She rushed back to town to tell her friends to come meet Jesus. He was the only one who could tell them how to have a new life, more satisfying than any water.

Mary and Martha

Mary was so excited. Jesus was coming to visit. Mary couldn't wait to talk with Jesus. There was nothing more wonderful to her.

Mary's sister, Martha, was excited too. But she was also nervous. There was so much to do before Jesus came. The house had to be cleaned. A big dinner had to be made. How would she do it all?

Soon Jesus came. Both sisters greeted Jesus warmly. Mary sat down by Jesus and was soon having a wonderful conversation with Him.

Martha hurried into the kitchen to check on the dinner. Then she quickly did more cleaning. She just couldn't sit down and relax. As Martha worked, she kept watching Mary and Jesus. They seemed to be having such a good talk. Finally Martha got a little bit angry.

"Mary," Martha said. "Why aren't you helping me with dinner? Why are you talking when we have work to do?"

Martha then walked over to Jesus. "Don't You think Mary should help me? It's not fair that she gets to talk with You while I do all the work."

Jesus smiled at Martha and gently said to her, "Martha, my dear friend. Please don't get upset over so many little things. What is most important is that we are together. Mary knows this."

Jesus was thankful, of course, for all Martha's work. But Jesus didn't visit to see how clean the house was, or to eat a good dinner. He came to spend time with His friends. And spending time with Jesus is the most important thing of all.

Jesus and the Children

It seemed that everyone wanted to be near Jesus. When He touched people, they became well. When He prayed, their hurts melted away. When He talked about God, it was so easy to see how to love one another. And what a wonderful storyteller He was!

One day some people heard that Jesus was going to be nearby. How excited they must have been. They couldn't wait to bring their children to Him. Some of the children may have been sick or crippled. Maybe Jesus could touch and heal them. Some of the children may have been sad. Maybe Jesus could pray and bring joy to their hearts. And some of the children may not have been behaving. Maybe Jesus could show them why it is so important to do what is right.

So the people hurried to Jesus with their children. As they came near, some of Jesus' disciples stopped them.

"May we see Jesus?" the people asked.

"He's too busy to see you," the disciples replied. "Now go away and don't bother Him." Can you imagine how sad the people must have felt?

But Jesus heard what His disciples said. He was not pleased at the way they talked to the people. Jesus called the children over to Him. He took them in His arms and held them. He talked with them and blessed them.

Then Jesus said to His disciples, "Never send children away! Anyone who wants to enter the kingdom of God must love and trust Me like little children do."

Zacchaeus Climbs a Tree

In the town of Jericho lived a man named Zacchaeus. Nobody liked him because he was a tax collector. He became very rich by making people pay more taxes than they were supposed to. Then he kept the extra money for himself.

One day Zacchaeus heard that Jesus was passing through his town. He really wanted to see Jesus. But Zacchaeus was a short man. How would he see over the crowd of people that was always around Jesus? Suddenly he had an idea! He ran down the road and climbed into the branches of a sycamore tree. Now he could see Jesus when He passed by.

Soon Zacchaeus saw a big crowd coming down the road toward him. Then Zacchaeus saw Jesus. But Zacchaeus was surprised when Jesus stopped right under the tree and looked up into the branches.

"Zacchaeus!" Jesus said to him. "Come down quickly. I want to go to your house today." Quickly Zacchaeus climbed down. He was happy to take Jesus to his house.

While Jesus talked with him, something happened to Zacchaeus. Suddenly he felt sad about cheating people. Jesus had changed Zacchaeus' heart. Now Zacchaeus wanted to do good. In fact, he promised to give half of all he owned to the poor. And if he had charged someone too much for taxes, he would give back four times as much.

This made Jesus very happy. It showed that Zacchaeus' life would be different now. Jesus told Zacchaeus, "Your soul was lost. But I came to find lost souls and save them."

A Wonderful Catch of Fish

People loved to listen to Jesus. One day, by the shore of the Sea of Galilee, so many people came to hear Him that they almost pushed Him into the water! Jesus looked around and saw two empty boats by the water's edge. One of them belonged to Simon Peter, a fisher who was mending his nets nearby. Jesus stepped into the boat and asked him to push it out into the water a little ways. Jesus could speak from there.

When Jesus finished teaching the people, He turned to Simon Peter and asked him to row the boat into deeper water. "Then let your nets down, and you will catch lots of fish," Jesus told him.

"Sir," Simon Peter answered Jesus, "we fished all night long. We worked very hard and didn't catch a thing. But we'll try again if you say so."

Simon Peter then threw his nets into the water once again. Suddenly the nets were so full of fish they began to tear. Simon Peter shouted to the other fishers on shore to come help him. Soon two boats were loaded with so many fish they almost sank!

When Simon Peter realized what Jesus had done, he was amazed. So were his partners, James and John. Simon Peter fell to his knees and cried to Jesus, "Sir, please leave us! I am too much of a sinner for You to be around."

Then Jesus calmed Simon Peter. He said, "Don't be afraid. I am making you a fisher of people's souls now." When they reached shore, Simon Peter and his friends left everything and went with Jesus.

A Young Man Comes Back to Life

One day Jesus and His friends went to the little village of Nain. But when they came into the village they saw something sad. There was a line of people, taking the body of a young man to bury.

And there was the young man's mother. She was a widow. Her husband had already died. Now her son, the only one who could take care of her, had died.

Jesus walked toward this funeral. What would He do? Would He say something kind to the woman? Would He try to comfort her? Instead Jesus told her not to weep, and He walked to the body of the young man. Everyone grew quiet now. What would He do?

Jesus pulled aside the sheet covering the young man's face. People began to whisper. Why did He do that?

"Young man," Jesus said. "Get up!" How could Jesus say that to a dead man? What did He expect this dead man to do?

The young man began to rise. The white sheet fell to the ground. The young man stood to his feet. He was alive! "He's alive!" people shouted. "He's alive!" Then the young man hugged his mother.

You can imagine how happy that mother was. You can imagine how many times she thanked Jesus for the wonderful miracle that He had done that day.

Jesus Quiets a Storm

I t had been a long, hard day. All morning and all afternoon people had crowded around Jesus. They wanted to hear Him talk about God's wonderful kingdom. They wanted Jesus to heal those who were sick. Jesus loved to be around people. But now He was tired. He needed some rest.

"Let's get in the boat and cross the lake to the other side," Jesus said to His disciples. Jesus went to the back of the boat and soon fell fast asleep.

Before long the wind began to blow hard. Dark clouds formed over the big lake. A big storm was coming.

It swept across the water with great speed. Soon giant waves spilled over the sides of the boat. It looked like the boat would tip over and sink! The disciples were afraid.

Jesus was still in the back of the boat, sound asleep. Some of the disciples rushed over to Him. They woke Him up shouting, "Master! We are about to drown. What can we do?"

Jesus woke up at once. He stood up, faced the terrible storm, and shouted, "Be still!" At once the wind died down and the storm stopped. All was quiet.

Jesus turned to the disciples and said, "Why were you so afraid? Don't you have faith in Me yet?"

The disciples were filled with awe. No ordinary person could do this. "Who can this be?" they asked. "Even the wind and waves obey Him." But they knew He was God's Son.

Jesus Feeds Five Thousand

Jesus climbed to the top of a large hill. Soon over 5,000 people gathered on the hillside around Jesus. Jesus talked with the people all day. They needed to know how to live in a way that pleases God.

Soon it would be dinnertime. Certainly the people were getting hungry. But they didn't want to leave Jesus.

Jesus turned to Philip and said, "Philip, where can we buy some food to feed these people?" Philip couldn't believe what Jesus was asking.

"It would take a fortune to buy enough food to feed all these people," he replied to Jesus. Andrew, Peter's brother, was nearby. He heard Jesus' question.

"There's a young boy here with five loaves of bread and two fish," he said. "But I suppose that won't feed 5,000 people!" The young boy was glad to give his bread and fish to Jesus.

Then Jesus said something that surprised the disciples. "Tell all the people to sit down." Jesus thanked God for the boy's food. Then He began to break off pieces of bread and fish and hand them to His disciples. He told the disciples to pass out the food to all the people. And do you know what? There was enough food for everyone! In fact, there was so much food left over that the scraps filled twelve full baskets.

"This is a great miracle!" the people said. They knew there was something very special about Jesus.

Jesus Walks on the Sea

"Take the boat to the other side of the Sea of Galilee," Jesus told His disciples. Jesus had preached to the crowds all day. Now He needed to rest and pray. He would join them later.

By the time it got dark, the disciples were halfway across the Sea of Galilee. Suddenly a strong wind began to blow, and they became caught in a storm. They rowed hard against the wind and waves, but they couldn't make any progress.

About four o'clock in the morning the disciples saw someone walking on the water right towards them! At first they thought it was a ghost. They screamed in fright.

But it was Jesus, and He quickly called out to comfort them. "Don't be afraid," He told them. "It is I, Jesus."

Then Peter called to Jesus, "If it really is You, let me walk on the water to You."

"All right," Jesus replied. "Come on."

So Peter jumped over the side of the boat and started walking to Jesus on top of the water. But then Peter looked at the high waves and became scared. As he started to sink, he called out to Jesus, "Save me!" Jesus was right there and reached out to take Peter's hand.

Jesus then said, "Peter, why did you doubt Me?" As they climbed into the boat the storm stopped.

The other disciples could hardly believe it all. "You really are God's Son," they exclaimed.

Jesus Heals Ten Lepers

"Unclean! Unclean!" some men shouted. "Lepers! Ten of them!" others whispered. "Stay away from them."

People did stay away from lepers. These were people with a bad disease called leprosy. Others were afraid of catching it. So they stayed away.

But Jesus did not stay away from the ten lepers. He was not afraid.

"Help us!" the ten lepers cried out to Jesus.

"Go to the priests," Jesus told the lepers. "Show them that you are clean."

The lepers knew what Jesus was saying. If they believed Him, they would be clean by the time they got to the priests. Then the priests would tell everyone they were clean.

People would not stay away from them any more.

So the lepers ran toward town to do what Jesus said. By the time they reached town their ugly spots were gone. They were clean.

Before long one of the ten came back to Jesus. "Thank You, thank You!" he said. "Thank You for healing me."

"Weren't there ten of you?" Jesus asked. "Where are the other nine?"

Jesus had healed ten men. But only one man remembered to thank Him.

Today, let us remember to thank Jesus for all He has done for us. Let us be like the one thankful man, not like the nine unthankful men.

The Good Samaritan

One day a man asked Jesus an important question. "What does a person have to do to live forever with God in heaven?"

Jesus asked him a question back. "What does the law of Moses say?"

The man thought for a moment and replied, "Love the Lord your God with all your heart, soul, and mind. And love your neighbor like yourself."

Jesus said, "You are right! If you love people like that, you will live forever."

But the man was not satisfied. There were some people he didn't want to love. What would Jesus say about them?

So he asked Jesus, "Who is my neighbor?"

Then Jesus told him a story about a Jewish man who went on a trip. Along the way the man was attacked by robbers. They beat him up and stole all his money.

Then they left him on the road, hurt and bleeding. After a while a Jewish priest came along. When he saw the poor man lying along the road, he passed to the other side and walked on by.

Later a Levite who worked at the Temple passed by. But he, too, ignored the bleeding man.

Then a Samaritan came along. Most Samaritans and Jews did not like each other. But this Samaritan stopped. He put bandages on the man's wounds. Then he put the man on his donkey and took him to the nearest inn.

"Please take care of this poor man until I return," he said. "I will pay whatever it costs."

After Jesus finished his story, the man knew that everyone was his neighbor and that he should help anyone in need.

The Lost Sheep

"Look at Jesus over there," some Pharisees said. They just couldn't understand why Jesus spent so much time with tax collectors and sinners. *They were bad people. Jesus should stay away from them,* the Pharisees thought. Jesus knew what those men were saying about Him. It was time for Jesus to tell them a story that would help them understand why He talked to those people.

Jesus went over to the Pharisees and said, "What if you owned 100 sheep and one of them got lost? Wouldn't you go out looking for that lost sheep? Wouldn't you search and search until you had found him?"

Of course we would, the Pharisees thought to themselves. They wondered what Jesus was trying to tell them.

Jesus continued His story. "Suppose you finally found this lost sheep," He said. "Wouldn't you be happy it had been found? Wouldn't you carry it home and have a great celebration? Wouldn't you be happy that the lost sheep was now safe at home?"

Then Jesus told the meaning of His story. He said, "When one lost sinner is brought back to God there is great joy in heaven. The lost sinner is part of God's family again. There is much happiness in heaven every time this happens."

Suddenly the Pharisees knew why Jesus spent so much time with sinners. He was trying to help them find God. He didn't want them to be lost sinners anymore. The Pharisees knew they should be doing the same thing.

The Young Man Who Ran Away

Two young men lived with their father in a beautiful home. They had everything they needed. But one son grew restless. He wanted to see the world.

One day this young man talked with his father. "You're going to die some day," he said. "You will leave part of your money to me. I want it now."

The father was sad to hear his son say that. But he gave the young man lots of money. Then the young man went away from home.

The young man thought he was rich. He bought lots of expensive things.

Before long the money was gone. He had spent it all.

Then a famine came to that land. He had no money to buy food. But there was no food to buy, even if he had money.

The young man tried to get a job. But the only work he could get was to feed a man's pigs. He was so hungry now that he wanted to eat the pigs' food.

One day the young man realized he had done a foolish thing. So he left for home. He would beg his father to forgive him.

As he came near his house his father saw him and ran to hug him. "We'll have a party!" the father said. "My lost son has been found." The father was so happy to have his son back. He forgave him and brought him back into the family. That's what God does to us when we ask Him.

Jesus' Triumphal Entry into Jerusalem

Jesus and His friends were near Bethany and Bethphage on the Mount of Olives. It was time for Him to go into Jerusalem. Now He would ride in on a donkey. In this way, Jesus would show people He was God's Son.

"Go into this village and you will find a colt tied," Jesus told some friends. "Bring it to Me. If anyone asks, tell him I need it."

The men found the colt. Some people asked what they were doing. They told them Jesus needed it. Then they brought the colt to Jesus. They put clothes on the colt's back and Jesus sat on it.

As Jesus rode toward Jerusalem, people ran out to meet Him. They cut branches and put them on the road where Jesus would ride. Some even put clothes on the road.

"Praise God!" people shouted. "Praise King David's descendant! Praise the one who comes in the name of the Lord."

Of course this stirred excitement in Jerusalem. Some religious leaders were angry. "Tell these people to stop saying such things," they told Jesus.

"If I do, these stones will cry out," Jesus answered.

Jesus rode on the donkey's colt into Jerusalem. Many years before, the prophet Zechariah had said this would happen. "Your king is coming, humble and riding on a donkey," he said. Jesus was greater than a king. He was God's Son.

Jesus at the Temple

When Jesus rode into Jerusalem He went to the temple. People were buying and selling things in the courtyard there. Moneychangers were trading their money for foreign money. People needed the moneychangers' money to buy things in the temple. But these money- changers cheated people. They charged more for their money than it was worth.

Others were selling doves. These were used in offerings to the Lord.

Jesus began to throw out the people who were selling. He turned over the moneychangers' tables. Their money spilled on the ground.

"My house is a house of prayer," Jesus said. "That is what the Bible says. But you have made it a house of thieves."

The temple leaders saw what Jesus did. They were angry. They wanted to kill Jesus.

Each day Jesus came to the temple. He taught the people about God. The people listened. They wanted to know what Jesus was saying.

The temple leaders could not hurt Jesus now. The people would not let them. They would have to wait.

At night Jesus left Jerusalem and went back to Bethany.

Jesus Teaches with Stories

"Who said You could do what You do?" some leaders asked Jesus one day. "Who said You could teach what You do?"

Jesus knew it was a trap. These people wanted Jesus to say something wrong. If He did, they would be able to kill Him.

What if Jesus said that God told Him to do these things? The leaders would say He claimed to be from God. That was called blasphemy. They could kill Him for that. What if He said someone else told Him to do these things? That wasn't good enough. Only God could tell someone what to do at the temple. No answer would be good enough. What should Jesus do?

"I will answer your question if you an-swer Mine," Jesus said. "Who told John the Baptist what to do?"

Now the leaders were trapped. If they said "God did," Jesus would ask why they didn't listen to John. If they said "someone else did," the people would be angry. The people thought God told John what to do.

"We don't know," said the leaders.

"Then I will not tell you who said I could do these things," Jesus answered.

Jesus began to teach the people with stories. We call these stories parables. They have two meanings. One is what the story says. The other is what the story tells about God and heaven. Jesus could teach many things through these stories.

A Coin for Caesar

One day some Pharisees and Herodians came to Jesus. They were religious leaders. They hated Jesus and wanted to kill Him. So they tried to trick Him.

"You are an honest man," they said to Jesus. "You teach the way about God truthfully. You are not worried about what people say about You. So tell us honestly. Is it right to pay taxes to Caesar or not?"

Jesus knew what they were doing. It was a mean, wicked trick to hurt Him. If Jesus said they should pay taxes it would make the people angry. These leaders could stir up the people against Him. If He said they should not pay taxes, it would make the Romans angry. The leaders would stir up the Romans against Jesus. What should He do?

"Why are you trying to trick Me?" Jesus asked. "Show Me a coin that you use to pay taxes."

The men found a coin and showed it to Jesus. "Whose picture and name are on this coin?" He asked.

"Caesar's," they answered. Caesar was the Roman emperor. The Romans ruled the land at that time.

"Give Caesar what belongs to Caesar," Jesus said. "Give God what belongs to God."

The men were amazed at what Jesus said. They did not know how to answer Him. So they left Him and went away.

The Widow's Mite

One day Jesus and His friends were in the temple. They were in a place called the treasury, where people gave their offerings. Money boxes were hanging on the wall around the room.

They watched people put money in the money boxes. Rich people dropped in lots of money. Then a poor widow came in. She dropped in two small copper coins, called mites. They were not even worth one cent today.

"Did you see how much the widow gave?" Jesus asked. They had seen how little she had given, not how much.

"That woman gave more than all the others," Jesus said. His friends must have looked surprised. How could Jesus say this? The woman had given only two small coins. Everyone else gave much more.

But Jesus kept on talking to them. "The others put in extra money they did not need," He said. "The poor widow put in all that she had. She needed those two coins for food and clothing."

Now Jesus' friends knew what He meant. It is not how much a person gives. It is how much a person keeps. The other people had given much. But they had kept more. The widow gave very little. But she kept nothing.

A Woman Anoints Jesus' Feet

Jesus was having dinner with Simon the leper. Simon lived in Bethany. This was the same town where Mary, Martha, and Lazarus lived.

While Jesus was eating, a woman came in with a jar of expensive perfumed oil. It was called nard. The woman opened the jar and poured the oil on Jesus while He ate.

The disciples were angry. "What a waste!" they complained. "This could have been sold for much money. We could have given that money to the poor."

Jesus heard what the disciples said. "Leave the woman alone," He said. "She did some-thing beautiful for Me. You will always have poor people with you. But you will not always have Me with you.

"This woman has put the perfumed oil on Me to help Me. She has prepared Me to be buried after I die." People put perfumed oil and spices on dead friends in those days.

Then Jesus said, "When the gospel is preached, the story of this woman will be told everywhere. People will remember what she has done."

This is true, isn't it? Perhaps you have heard a sermon about this woman.

Judas Takes Thirty Pieces of Silver

Judas Iscariot was one of Jesus' twelve special helpers. Judas had been with Jesus for a long time. He had heard Jesus teach and watched His miracles. But he did not truly love Jesus. He loved money more than Jesus.

That is why Judas went to see the chief priests. These people wanted to kill Jesus. Now Judas would help them.

"What will you pay me to betray Jesus?" Judas asked. He was offering to help them capture his friend. He would sell his friend to these men for money.

"Thirty pieces of silver," the men answered. So they counted thirty silver coins and gave them to Judas. They were glad to pay Judas this money. They would pay lots of money to capture Jesus and kill Him. These men were jealous of the things Jesus did. They wanted people to follow them instead of following Jesus.

Judas took the money. He would betray Jesus for thirty silver coins. When he left, he began to look for a time and place to betray Jesus.

Preparing for the Last Supper

The time had come for the Passover, when the lambs were killed for the Passover supper. This was also called the Feast of Unleavened Bread. Jesus asked two of his disciples to get their Passover supper ready. This supper would be their last supper together. We remember it today when we have Communion. Sometimes we call the supper they ate together the Last Supper.

"Will you do this for us?" Jesus asked them.

"Where should we eat?" they asked.

"When you go into Jerusalem, you will meet a man carrying a pitcher of water," Jesus said. "Follow him to the house where he is going. Ask the owner about our room. He will show you a large upstairs room. You will get that room ready for our supper."

The disciples went into Jerusalem. Everything happened the way Jesus said it would. They met a man with a pitcher of water. They followed the man to a house and asked the owner about a room. The owner showed them the room where they would eat the supper together.

The disciples got the Passover supper ready. Now Jesus and His friends could eat it together. Now they would have a pleasant room for the Last Supper.

The Last Supper

The two disciples had prepared the food for the Passover supper. Now it was evening, and Jesus had come. His twelve special helpers were there too. It was time to eat the supper in the upstairs room.

While they were eating, Jesus said, "One of you will betray Me." The disciples were sad to hear this.

"Am I the one?" each asked.

"The one who dips his bread in the dish with Me is the one," Jesus answered. "I must die, but for the man who betrays Me, it would be better if he had not been born."

Jesus took some bread and thanked God for it. Then He broke it and gave it to His friends.

"Take this and eat it," Jesus said. "This bread is My body."

Then Jesus took a cup and thanked God for it. He gave the cup to His friends. "This is My blood," He said. "It is poured out for many people to forgive their sins. I will not drink any more of this until I drink it with you in God's Kingdom."

When the supper was over, Jesus and His friends sang a hymn. Then they left for a place called Gethsemane.

Jesus Prays in Gethsemane

After the Last Supper Jesus left Jerusalem with His disciples. He went through the Kidron Valley to the Mount of Olives, just east of the temple.

Jesus took His disciples to a quiet grove of olive trees called Gethsemane. They had come here often. "Sit here while I pray," Jesus said.

Jesus took Peter, James, and John a short distance away. "I am very sad and full of sorrow," Jesus told them. "I am almost crushed with grief and pain. Stay here and watch with Me."

Then Jesus went a few feet away and bowed His face toward the ground. "Father, if it is possible, take this suffering from Me," He said. "But do whatever You want." An angel came and strengthened Him, and He prayed some more.

And Jesus had great drops of sweat as if He were bleeding.

When Jesus came back to Peter, James, and John, they were asleep. "Could you not watch with Me one hour?" Jesus asked Peter. "You should watch so you will not fall because of temptation. You want to do what is right, but your body is weak."

Jesus went away and prayed a second time. When He came back His disciples were asleep again.

Then He went away and prayed a third time. And when He came back the disciples were still sleeping.

"Get up!" Jesus said. "The time has come for Me to be turned over to sinners. Here comes the person who is betraying Me."

Judas led a mob to Gethsemane. He knew where Jesus would be.

Judas Betrays Jesus

Jesus was in Gethsemane with His friends. He saw Judas coming with a mob. Judas knew Jesus would be here. He often came here with His friends, the disciples. Now Judas was bringing soldiers and guards from the religious leaders. They carried swords and clubs and torches.

Judas had given the mob a signal. The man I kiss is Jesus, he had told them.

Judas went to Jesus and said, "Teacher!"

Judas kissed Jesus. "Friend, why have you come?" Jesus said to Judas. Then some men came toward Jesus. "Who do you want?" Jesus asked.

"Jesus," they answered.

"I am Jesus," He said. The soldiers and guards fell to the ground. Then Jesus asked again, "Who do you want?"

"Jesus," they said.

"I told you I am Jesus," He said. "Why are you coming here for Me? I have taught each day in the temple."

Peter had a sword. He struck Malchus, a servant of the high priest and cut off the man's right ear.

"Put that away," Jesus told Peter. "I could ask My Father, and He would send, twelve armies of angels. This must happen because the Bible said it would." Then all of Jesus' disciples ran away. Someone grabbed a young man's cloak and pulled it off. He fled naked.

Jesus Is Tried

When the soldiers and guards took Jesus to Jerusalem, they led Him to Annas. He had been the high priest. Now Caiaphas, his son-in-law, was the high priest.

Annas asked Jesus about His followers and His teachings. "I have taught in the open," Jesus said. "Ask the people who heard Me."

A guard slapped Jesus. "How dare You talk to the high priest like that!" he said.

Annas sent Jesus to Caiaphas. Jesus' hands were tied. The religious leaders were waiting there. They tried to find something wrong with Jesus. But they couldn't. Many told lies about Jesus. Two men said, "He claimed that He could build the temple in three days if it was torn down."

Jesus was quiet all the time. "Won't You answer?" Caiaphas demanded. "Tell me, are You the Messiah, God's Son?"

"It is as you say," said Jesus. "Some day you will see Me at God's right hand, coming on the clouds of heaven."

Caiaphas tore his robe. "Blasphemy!" he shouted. "We don't need more witnesses. What do you think?"

"He must die," the other religious leaders said.

Some spat in Jesus' face. Some slapped Him. "Who hit You?" they mocked. "Tell us like a prophet."

Peter Denies Jesus

When the soldiers and guards took Jesus to Caiaphas' house, Peter went quietly into the courtyard. He stood with the servants, who warmed themselves by a charcoal fire.

Before long, a servant girl of the high priest stared at Peter. "You were with Jesus," she said.

"I don't know what you are talking about," Peter said. He left and went into a gateway. Then a rooster crowed.

While Peter was in the gateway another servant girl saw him. "He was with Jesus," she said. But Peter denied it.

About an hour later a man said, "You can't deny that you were with Jesus. You talk with a Galilean accent."

"I swear that I am telling the truth," Peter shouted. "I don't know what you are talking about." Peter began to curse. At that moment Jesus was led by. He stared at Peter.

Suddenly Peter remembered what Jesus had said earlier. "Before the rooster crows, you will deny Me three times," Jesus had told him.

Peter ran out of the courtyard. He cried as if his heart was broken.

Judas Hangs Himself

Judas Iscariot had betrayed Jesus for thirty silver coins. He had taken soldiers and guards to Gethsemane. He had kissed Jesus to show them the One to capture.

Now Judas learned that Jesus was going to die. Judas was sorry for what he had done. He took the thirty silver coins to the religious leaders.

"I have sinned," he told them. "I have betrayed an innocent man and caused Him to die."

"So what?" they said. "That is your problem."

Judas threw the coins on the temple floor. He ran away and hanged himself. Then he slipped from the place he was hanging and his body burst open.

The religious leaders picked up the coins. "We can't put this with the temple money," they said. "Our rules will not let us do that. It is money that has bought a person's death."

After they talked about it, they decided to buy potter's field, a place to bury strangers. It was called the Field of Blood, or Akel Dama.

The prophet Jeremiah had written about this 600 years before. "They took thirty silver coins, which they said they would pay for Him," said Jeremiah. "They bought a potter's field, as the Lord said."

Jesus Is Crucified

"**N**ail Him to the cross," the Roman officer shouted. Roman soldiers nailed Jesus' hands and feet to the wooden cross. Then they set the cross up so people could watch Him die.

Near the cross, Roman soldiers threw some dice. They wanted Jesus' robe. It was like "drawing straws" to see who would get it. Jesus' mother and friends were there too. They were very sad to watch Jesus die. The sky grew very dark. The earth shook and groaned. Rocks burst in two. Dead people got up and walked around. God was showing people that Jesus was His Son.

The Romans ruled the land of Israel in Jesus' time. To them, crucifixion was much like the electric chair is today. It was their way of executing criminals.

But Jesus was not a criminal. The religious leaders had accused Him falsely. They hated Jesus. People were following Jesus instead of them. So they wanted to kill Jesus.

Jesus hung on the cross most of that day. Then He died. He died so that you and I could have our sins forgiven.

Jesus Is Raised from the Dead

Early on Sunday morning Mary Magdalene, Mary, the mother of James and Salome went to the tomb. That's where Jesus had been laid on Friday. They wanted to put some spices on His body. That's the way people did it at that time.

"Look," one of the women said. "The stone is rolled away from the tomb." They ran to see what had happened. But when they came to the tomb, they stopped and cried out. Two men stood by them.

"Don't be afraid," they said "Jesus isn't here. He is risen!"

Jesus certainly was not in the tomb now. So the women ran to tell the disciples. This was good news. It was the best news they had heard for a long time. Jesus had come back to life. He had risen!

Each Easter we sing wonderful songs about this morning long ago. We sing about Jesus, who arose from the dead. That shows us that He controls life and death.

The Holy Spirit Comes at Pentecost

Seven weeks after Jesus died and arose from the dead, His followers met together. It was a special holiday called the Day of Pentecost.

Suddenly they heard a roaring sound, like a great wind blowing through the house where they met. Little flames of fire came upon each person's head. Then each person began speaking a foreign language. The Holy Spirit gave the people the power to do this.

There were some people nearby who knew these languages. They were from the countries where the languages were spoken. They were amazed, for they knew Jesus' followers did not really know these foreign languages.

"How can this be?" they asked.

"These people are drunk!" some said.

But Peter gave a speech to the crowd.

"The prophet Joel said this would happen. Many years ago he said that God would pour out His Spirit on the people," Peter said.

About 3,000 people believed what Peter said and were baptized that day. With Jesus' other followers they met to listen to the apostles teach. They also met for prayer meetings and communion services.

Some of these believers sold what they owned and divided the money with other believers who needed it.

How thankful and happy Jesus' followers were as they met together in God's house, the temple, each day. They held small meetings together in other places, and they praised God for all that was happening. No wonder their neighbors seemed pleased with these people! Perhaps that is why more and more believers were added each day.

Peter and John Heal a Lame Man

It was time for the three o'clock worship service at the temple, God's house. Peter and John were going there to pray when they saw a crippled man beside the Beautiful Gate. The, man who was brought there every day, asked Peter and John for money. Peter and John stopped to talk to him.

"Look at us!" said Peter. The man looked, expecting some money.

"We have no money to give you," said Peter. "But we have another gift. In the name of Jesus, get up and walk!"

Peter took the man by the hand and lifted him to his feet. Suddenly the man's feet were healed, and he began to leap and walk. Then he began to jump around, praising God. He even ran into God's house.

You can imagine how surprised people were to see the crippled beggar jumping around. But Peter said, "Why are you so surprised? We didn't do this. God did this so He could honor Jesus. This is the same Jesus that you killed in ignorance. But we have seen Him alive. Now He wants you to turn away from your sins."

Peter and John Before the Council

One day Peter gave a speech. He reminded the people that they had killed Jesus, even though He was God's Son. But Jesus was alive, for He had risen from the dead.

While Peter talked, the chief priests, the captain of the temple police, and some Sadducees came closer. What Peter and John were saying disturbed them, especially that Jesus arose from the dead. So they had Peter and John put in jail.

Many of the people who had listened to Peter that day believed in Jesus. By this time there were about 5,000 believers.

The next day Peter and John were brought before the council of Jewish leaders meeting in Jerusalem. There were a number of the highest officials there, including Annas, the high priest, and some of his relatives. When Peter and John were brought in, some council members demanded, "By whose authority are you doing these things?"

Peter was filled with the Holy Spirit when he answered, "In the name and power of Jesus, God's Son, whom you crucified."

The council members could see that Peter and John were uneducated men, but here they were preaching boldly. They knew these men had been with Jesus.

The council decided to warn Peter and John. But the two men answered, "We can't stop talking about Jesus, for we must do what God wants, not what you want."

When Peter and John went back to the other believers, they all had a prayer meeting. Then the building shook and the Holy Spirit came upon them again. After that, Jesus' followers became even more courageous in preaching about Jesus.

People Who Believed in Jesus

Wonderful things were happening in Jerusalem. In less than two months since Jesus was crucified and arose from the dead, 5,000 had accepted Him as Savior. They were called believers. Those believers were united in heart and mind.

The apostles were preaching great sermons about Jesus' rising from the dead. And the believers were gathering together to help one another and to enjoy one another's company. Many believers sold their houses and lands and gave the money to those who needed it.

Joseph, also called Barnabas, did this. Ananias and his wife, Sapphira, also sold some land, and Ananias brought part of the money to Peter. Ananias pretended that it was all of the money. He and Sapphira had agreed to this scheme.

Peter said to Ananias, "You are lying to the Holy Spirit. That was your property, and when you sold it, that was your money. But why did you lie to God about what you gave?" Ananias fell to the floor and was dead. Some young men covered him with a cloth and took him outside to bury him.

Sapphira came to see Peter about three hours later. "Did you sell your land for this amount?" Peter asked.

"Yes," said Sapphira. She also lied to God.

"How could you and your husband do this?" Peter asked. "The young men who buried your husband are waiting to bury you, too."

Then Sapphira fell to the floor dead, and the young men carried her out and buried her next to her husband. Of course the whole church was afraid when the people heard this.

The Seven Deacons

As time passed, more people became believers in Jesus. They accepted Him as their Savior and joined the others who had accepted Him too.

But as the number of believers grew, the problems among them grew. Before long, some of these people began to complain. The believers who spoke Greek thought their widows were not getting as much food as the widows of those who spoke Hebrew.

At that time, the apostles were giving food to needy people each day. The apostles did not like this grumbling, and so they called a meeting of the believers.

"We're spending too much time distributing food," the apostles told the believers. "We should be spending our time preaching. You must choose some other people to distribute the food so we can preach. Choose seven men who are wise and filled with the Holy Spirit. Be sure the other believers think well of them. We will let them do the work of distributing food. Then we will give our time to pray, preach, and teach."

The believers thought this was a good idea, and so they chose the following seven men: Stephen, who was an unusual man of faith and filled with the Holy Spirit, Philip, Prochorus, Nicanor, Timon, Parmenas, and Nicolas of Antioch. Nicolas had been a Gentile at first but had become a Jewish convert. And then he had become a believer in Jesus as Savior.

The seven, sometimes called deacons, were brought to the apostles. Then the apostles put their hands upon them and prayed for them. This was a way of asking God to bless their work.

Stephen Is Stoned

Stephen was filled with faith and the power of the Holy Spirit. He did amazing miracles among the people. Of course there were some people who did not like this preaching and miracle-working.

One day, some members of "The Freedmen," a Jewish cult, began to argue with Stephen. Some other Jewish men joined in. Stephen was so wise and had such a wonderful way about him that no one could find anything wrong with him. So these men found some wicked fellows to lie about Stephen. They said he had cursed Moses and God.

These lying men stirred up the crowds against Stephen so the Jewish leaders arrested him and had him taken to the Council. This was the court where the leaders decided what to do with people like Stephen.

The lying men told the Council that Stephen was saying terrible things about the temple, God's house, and God's laws. When the members of the Council looked at Stephen, they saw that his face glowed like an angel's face.

"Are these things true?" the high priest asked Stephen.

Stephen gave a long speech to the Council. "Your ancestors killed the prophets, and you killed God's Son," he told them. These leaders were furious. The leaders and their people dragged Stephen out of the city of Jerusalem. Then they took off their cloaks and laid them at the feet of a young man named Saul. Later he would become the apostle Paul, but now he was one of those killing Stephen. Then these people threw stones at Stephen until he died.

"Lord, let me go to be with You," Stephen prayed. "And please don't punish these men for their sin." When Stephen said that, he fell asleep.

Philip Preaches in Samaria

When Stephen was stoned to death, a wave of persecution began against the believers. It moved across the Jerusalem church, and all but the apostles ran away into Judea and Samaria.

Even though this happened, some godly men risked their lives to come and bury Stephen. Saul went around like a wild animal, trying to hurt the believers. He went into believers' houses and dragged men and women to prison.

The believers who had escaped from Jerusalem preached the good news about Jesus everywhere. Philip went to the city of Samaria to tell people there about Jesus.

Crowds came to hear Philip. They listened carefully, for Philip also did many miracles. Evil spirits were cast out, shouting as they left each person. Even the paralyzed and crippled were healed. All of this brought much joy to the city.

A sorcerer named Simon lived in Samaria. The people were so impressed with Simon's magic that they often spoke of this proud man as the messiah, God's son. But when the people heard Philip, they believed that Jesus was God's Son and were baptized. Even Simon believed and was baptized. He followed Philip and watched his miracles with amazement.

The Jerusalem believers heard what was happening and sent Peter and John to Samaria for a report. These men prayed for the new believers and put their hands on them, and they received the Holy Spirit. Simon wanted to do this too, so he offered to buy this power from the apostles.

"Your heart is not right with God," Peter told Simon. "You can't buy this power. Turn from your evil and ask God to forgive your sin."

"Pray for me," Simon begged.

Philip and the Ethiopian

One day an angel of the Lord appeared to Philip with an important message. "Leave Samaria now and go south to the desert road that runs from Jerusalem to Gaza," the angel said.

When Philip came to this place, he saw a chariot coming. The treasurer of Ethiopia sat in the chariot, coming from the temple in Jerusalem. He had been there to worship God and was now on his way home. As this man rode along in the chariot, he read aloud from a scroll. It was the book of Isaiah.

"Run beside this chariot," the Holy Spirit told Philip. Philip quickly obeyed.

"Do you understand what you are reading?" Philip asked.

"No, I don't," said the man. "How can I understand without someone to help me?" Then the man asked Philip to come into the chariot and sit with him. Philip saw that the man was reading about a sheep going to the slaughter and a lamb remaining silent before the shearers.

"Was Isaiah writing about himself or someone else?" the man asked Philip.

Philip started with the words of Isaiah and taught this man about Jesus. He showed him many other Scriptures about Jesus too.

"Why can't I be baptized?" the man asked. Philip could see that the man believed in Jesus now, so they stopped. Philip and the man went into some water by the road and Philip baptized him.

When they came out of the water, the Spirit of God took Philip away, and the Ethiopian did not see where he went. But the Ethiopian went home, filled with joy.

Saul Is Converted

Saul was getting worse in his persecution of the believers. One day he went to the high priest and asked to go to the synagogues of Damascus. Saul wanted to find believers there and put them in prison. But when he went near Damascus, a light shone around him from heaven. Saul fell to the ground.

"Saul, why are you hurting Me like this?" a voice from heaven asked.

"Who are you, Lord?" Saul asked.

"I am Jesus. You are hurting Me," the voice said. "Get up and go into Damascus. You will be told what to do."

When Saul got up, he realized he was blind. So his companions led him to Damascus, where he remained blind for three days.

Meanwhile, in Damascus, a believer named Ananias had a vision. "Go to the house of Judas on Straight Street and ask for Saul of Tarsus," God told Ananias. "He is waiting for you."

Ananias was afraid. "But he is a terrible man," Ananias argued.

"Do what I tell you," God said. "I have chosen Saul to be a special missionary. He must suffer many things for Me."

Ananias went and found Saul. He put his hands on him and said, "Jesus has sent me to do this so you will be filled with the Holy Spirit and can see again." Just as if scales fell from his eyes, Saul could see again. Then he was baptized.

After Saul ate he got his strength again. Saul stayed there with the believers of Damascus a few days. He went to the syn- agogue at Damascus to tell them that Jesus is God's Son. The people at the synagogue were quite surprised to hear Saul preach like this. "Isn't this the man who hurt so many believers in Jerusalem?" they asked.

Saul Escapes in a Basket

Saul had hated the people who believed in Jesus. He had hurt many of them. He even went to Damascus to hurt Jesus' followers there. But on the way, Jesus spoke to him from heaven. Saul accepted Jesus as his Savior too.

Now Saul was preaching about Jesus. He even went into the synagogues and preached to his old friends. Of course this surprised them. Before long, they grew angry and planned to kill Saul. But Saul heard about this plot.

Each day and each night these men watched the gates of Damascus to catch Saul when he went out. They would kill him. But Saul's new friends, those who believed in Jesus, put Saul in a basket one night. Then they let him down through an opening in the wall.

Saul escaped to Jerusalem, but Jesus' followers were afraid to accept him. Then Barnabas told the apostles how Saul had accepted Jesus and how he had preached with much courage in Damascus. Now the believers accepted Saul, and he worked with them in Jerusalem.

Before long, some enemies tried to kill Saul, so the believers took him to the seaport at Caesarea and sent him to his hometown of Tarsus.

Peter Heals Aeneas

eter traveled through the country, visiting Jesus' followers in different places. One day he stopped in Lydda. Peter met Aeneas there, a man who had been paralyzed for eight years. Aeneas was so crippled that he had to stay in bed all the time.

"Jesus Christ has healed you, Aeneas!" Peter said to him. "Get up and make your bed." Aeneas believed what Peter said. He got up immediately.

All the neighbors in Lydda and even those in the surrounding countryside of Sharon were amazed. When they saw what happened to Aeneas, many of them also believed in Jesus.

Peter Raises Dorcas from the Dead

Tabitha was a wonderful Christian woman who was always helping the poor. Some people called her Dorcas, which meant *gazelle*. Perhaps that was because she was always running around doing special things for people. Dorcas lived in Joppa, just a few miles northwest of Lydda, where Peter had healed Aeneas.

After Dorcas died, her friends washed her body and laid it in an upstairs room. Then they sent two men to Peter. "Come quickly," they urged.

When Peter came to the house, Dorcas's friends took him upstairs to the place where they had put her body. Widows gathered around Peter, crying as they showed him all the cloaks and other clothing Dorcas had made for them. Peter asked everyone to leave the room. Then he knelt and prayed.

"Get up!" he said to Dorcas. Suddenly she opened her eyes, looked at Peter, and sat up. Peter took her by the hand and lifted her up. Then he called the widows and other believers in and presented her to them alive.

Before long, the news of this miracle spread all over Joppa. Many believed in Jesus because of this.

Cornelius Becomes a Christian

One day a Roman army centurion named Cornelius had a vision. He was a godly man in charge of a regiment of soldiers. While Cornelius prayed he saw an angel and heard him speak. "Cornelius!" the angel said.

"What do you want, Lord?" Cornelius answered.

"God wants you to send two men for Peter, who is staying with Simon at Joppa."

As these men were drawing near Joppa the next day, Peter went up to Simon's roof to pray. Suddenly he saw a big sheet, with animals, reptiles, and birds in it. "Kill and eat them," God told Peter.

"No!" said Peter. "These are unclean according to our religious laws. I've never eaten those kinds of things."

"But if I have made something clean, you must not call it unclean," God said.

This happened three times. Then the sheet went away. As soon as that happened the men arrived from Cornelius's house. The Holy Spirit spoke to Peter and told him to go with them.

When Peter went into the house, Cornelius bowed to the floor. "Stand up," said Peter. "I am only a man."

According to Jewish law, Peter should not have been in Cornelius's house, for Cornelius was a Gentile. A Gentile was someone who had not been born a Jew and who did not follow their religious laws. But when Cornelius told Peter about his vision from God and accepted Jesus as Savior, Peter knew God had sent him.

Believers at Antioch Called Christians

When Peter returned to Jerusalem, the Jewish believers criticized him for visiting Cornelius and eating with his friends and relatives. They had already heard about this, and they had heard how the Gentiles had accepted Jesus as their Savior.

Then Peter explained the whole story to them. He told them about his vision, and how Cornelius had also had a vision from God. When they heard this, they were glad and stopped their criticism.

About the same time more Gentiles were accepting Jesus as Savior at Antioch. The church at Jerusalem sent Barnabas there to see what was happening. When he saw how God was working, he encouraged the believers there to keep on with their good work.

Then he went to Tarsus, found Saul, and brought him back to Antioch to work. Barnabas and Saul stayed there for a year, working with the church at Antioch. It was there that believers were first called Christians.

While Barnabas and Saul were at Antioch, a prophet named Agabus came with some other prophets from Jerusalem. He predicted a famine would spread over the Roman Empire, and it actually happened during the time when Claudius was emperor.

The Christians at Antioch decided they would take a collection for the Christians in Judea and Jerusalem. So they did this and sent it there with Barnabas and Saul.

Peter Is Put into Prison and Escapes

King Herod began to arrest the Christians and persecute them. He executed John's brother, James, with a sword. He put Peter in prison and put a guard of four squads of four soldiers each to watch him. After the Passover, he would put Peter on trial.

The Christians began to pray earnestly while Peter was in prison. The night before Peter would go on trial, he was sleeping between two soldiers, bound by chains. Soldiers guarded the entrance. Suddenly an angel of the Lord appeared and a light shone in the prison cell. The angel struck Peter's side to wake him.

"Get up!" the angel said. Then the chains fell from Peter's wrists. "Put on your clothes and sandals," the angel said. "Follow me."

Peter did what the angel said and followed him from the prison. The iron gate opened and they walked down the street. Then the angel disappeared.

Peter headed for the house of Mary, John Mark's mother. Christians were praying there for Peter. Peter knocked on the courtyard door and a servant girl named Rhoda answered. She knew it was Peter's voice and was so happy that she ran to tell the others. Rhoda was so excited she forgot to open the door.

"Peter is at the door!" she cried out.

"You're crazy," the others said. "It must be his angel." But she insisted that he was there, and Peter kept on knocking. At last they let him in. Then Peter had them be quiet. After he told them what had happened, he left.

There was quite a stir the next day at the prison. Herod executed the guards, then went to Caesarea where he put on royal robes and gave a speech.

"This is a god!" some people shouted. Herod accepted their praise, but God was angry and struck him down with worms so that he died.

Paul Begins His Travels for Jesus

"I have a special work for Barnabas and Saul," the Holy Spirit said. The Christians at Antioch prayed and put their hands on these two men. Then they sent them on a trip. These men would tell people in other countries about Jesus. John Mark went with them.

They went to Seleucia, Cyprus, Salamis, and Paphos. The governor of Paphos, Sergius Paulus, invited the men to tell him about Jesus. But a magician named Elymas tried to keep the governor from believing.

"You are working against God," Paul told him. "God will make you blind for a while." Suddenly Elymas was blind, begging for someone to lead him.

The next stop was Perga. For some reason John Mark left Paul and Barnabas and went home to Jerusalem.

Paul and Barnabas went on to Antioch in Pisidia. On the Sabbath they went to the synagogue. Paul preached a sermon about Jesus. "He is the Messiah, God's Son," Paul said.

Paul and Barnabas went back the next Sabbath. Almost everyone in town went too. But the Jews were jealous when they saw the big crowd. They argued with Paul and insulted him.

"We had to bring the good news to you first," Paul told them. "But you have rejected it. Now we will take it to the Gentiles." The Gentiles were glad to hear this. Many of them believed. Then the Jews stirred up trouble and made Paul and Barnabas leave town.

Paul and Barnabas Are Mistaken for Gods

There was a crippled man in Lystra who had never walked. While Paul preached, the man listened. Paul watched and knew he could be healed.

"Stand on your feet!" Paul shouted.

The man jumped up and walked. This was an amazing miracle. The people of Lystra began to shout, "The gods have come to us. They look like men, but they are gods."

The people called Paul "Hermes" and they called Barnabas "Zeus." There was a temple of Zeus just outside town. The priest brought bulls and flowers. He and the people wanted to offer these to Paul and Barnabas as a sacrifice.

Paul and Barnabas tore their clothes when they saw this. "Why are you doing this?" they said. "We are only people, like you. We are here to tell you the good news about Jesus."

The people of Lystra still wanted to make a sacrifice to them.

Then some men came from Antioch. Others came from Iconium. They said bad things about Paul and Barnabas. The people of Lystra believed them. Then they threw stones at Paul and dragged him out of town. They thought he was dead.

But the Christians came to help Paul. He got up and went back into Lystra. The next day he and Barnabas went on to Derbe.

Paul Is Called to Macedonia

Paul and Barnabas had an argument. Barnabas wanted John Mark to come with them again. Paul did not want him. So Barnabas chose John Mark to go with him. Paul chose Silas to go with him.

Paul and Silas went through Derbe to Lystra. A believer named Timothy lived there. He had a Jewish mother and a Greek father. All the Christians in Lystra and Iconium said good things about Timothy.

Paul wanted to take Timothy with him. So he circumcised him. The Jews in the towns where they were going knew Timothy's father was Greek. They would not accept him unless he was circumcised.

Paul, Timothy, and Silas traveled from town to town. They met with the believers. They told the believers what the apostles and elders in Jerusalem had decided. They told them the rules for the new churches. These churches grew stronger and larger each day.

Paul and his friends went through Phrygia and Galatia. The Holy Spirit did not let them preach in the area called Asia.

One night at the town of Troas, Paul had a vision. In the vision a Macedonian man begged, "Come over to Macedonia and help us."

Paul was sure that this was God's way of telling them what to do. So he and his friends got ready to go.

Timothy's Family and Home

Timothy was a wonderful young man. He lived in Lystra. This is in the country of Turkey today.

Timothy's father was a Gentile, a Greek man. His mother, Eunice, was Jewish.

Eunice was a godly woman. But then so was Eunice's mother, Lois. They must have told Timothy many stories about Abraham, Isaac, Joseph, and David when he grew up. They prayed with him and helped him love God.

Someone told Timothy about Jesus. It was probably Paul who did this. Timothy learned that Jesus was God's Son. He accepted Jesus as his Savior.

When Paul came to Lystra he heard people talk about this wonderful young man. Paul wanted Timothy to go with him to other towns. He would help Paul tell others about Jesus.

Paul circumcised Timothy. The Jewish people would accept him then. After that Timothy went with Paul to help him.

Many years later, not long before he died, Paul wrote two letters to Timothy. They are in our Bibles. In these letters, Paul said that Timothy was like a son to him. He prayed for Timothy day and night. He knew that Timothy was a man of God. He begged Timothy to keep true to God.

Would you like to be like Timothy?

Lydia Becomes a Christian

aul and his friends went from Troas to Macedonia by ship. Their first stop was the island of Samothrace. Then they sailed for the seaport called Neapolis. From there they walked to Philippi.

Philippi was the most important city of that part of Macedonia. It was also a Roman colony.

Paul and his friends stayed several days at Philippi. On the Sabbath they went to the riverside outside town. They thought they would find some Jews gathered there for prayer.

There was a group of women by the river. One of them was Lydia, who sold purple cloth. She believed in God and worshiped Him.

Lydia listened carefully to Paul. She believed in Jesus and asked Paul to baptize her and the other people in her house.

"Stay with us in my house," Lydia told Paul and his friends. "If you think I'm truly a Christian, please stay."

Paul and his friends stayed with Lydia at her house. It was good to have a home and food in a strange place. Paul and his friends must have been thankful, don't you think?

The Prison at Philippi

Paul and his friends stayed several days at Philippi. One day as they were going to pray a slave girl met them. She had an evil spirit in her. The girl's owners made much money because this girl was a fortune-teller.

"In Jesus' name, I command you to come out of that girl!" Paul shouted. The evil spirit came out at that moment.

The girl's owners were angry. They knew they could not make money with the girl now. So they grabbed Paul and Silas and dragged them to the town officials in the public square. "These Jews are causing trouble here," they said. "They are teaching things against our law. We cannot let them do this." Soon the crowd that had gathered was against Paul and Silas.

The officials tore the clothes from Paul and Silas. They had them beaten and thrown into the inner prison with large blocks of wood fastened to their feet.

About midnight Paul and Silas were praying and singing. The other prisoners listened. Suddenly an earthquake shook the prison. The doors opened, and the chains fell from the prisoners. When the jailer saw this he tried to kill himself. He would be tortured if he let these men escape.

"Don't hurt yourself." Paul said. "We are all here."

Then the jailer rushed in with a light, he fell down before Paul and Silas. He was trembling. "What must I do to be saved?" he asked.

"Believe in the Lord Jesus," Paul answered. "Then you and your family will be saved." Paul then told the jailer and the others in his house about Jesus.

The jailer washed their wounds. Then he and his family were baptized. The jailer and his family were happy now because they were Christians.

The Bereans Accept Paul

Wherever Paul went, someone tried to hurt him. There were many people who did not want others to believe in Jesus.

When Paul visited Thessalonica, the same thing happened. Some people stirred up the crowd around them. They got Paul and his friends in a lot of trouble.

The Christians at Thessalonica sent Paul and his friends to Berea one night. Paul went to the synagogue to preach, as he always did in a town.

The people at Berea listened carefully to Paul. They were not against him like others had been. Each day they studied the Bible to see if the things Paul said were true.

Many of the people of Berea became Christians. Some of these new Christians were important Greek men and women.

But Paul's enemies in Thessalonica came to Berea. They stirred up trouble. So the Christians in Berea sent Paul to the coast. Silas and Timothy stayed in Berea a while.

Some Bereans went with Paul as far as Athens, in Greece. When they came back to Berea, they brought a message from Paul. "Come and join me as soon as possible," Paul told Silas and Timothy.

Paul at Mars Hill

Paul was waiting in Athens for Silas and Timothy. As he looked around the city he became upset at the many idols he saw.

At the synagogue, Paul talked to Jews and Greeks who worshiped God. He also went to the marketplace each day to talk with the people there.

Some Epicurean and Stoic teachers argued with Paul. But he told them the good news, how Jesus rose from the dead.

"He's dreaming," they said. "He doesn't know what he is saying. He must be teaching about some foreign religion."

These men took Paul to Mars Hill. It was also called Areopagus. The city council was there. These men wanted to hear what Paul was saying. "We want to know what these things mean," they said. People in Athens spent most of their time talking about new things.

Paul spoke to the city council. "You people of Athens are very religious," he said. "You even have an altar to an unknown god." Then Paul talked about God and His Son Jesus.

When the people of Athens heard Paul talk about Jesus' being raised from the dead, some made fun of him. Others asked to hear him again. One council member became a Christian, along with a woman named Damaris, and some others.

Books of Magic Are Burned

While Paul lived in Ephesus, God did some wonderful miracles through him. People put some of Paul's clothes or handkerchiefs on sick people. These people were healed or evil spirits left them.

At that time there were people who traveled around, making evil spirits go out of people. Now they tried to do this by using Jesus' name like a charm.

The seven sons of Sceva were doing this. "I order you out by Jesus, the person Paul talks about," they would say.

One time they tried this with a man. The evil spirit in him said, "I know Jesus and Paul, but who are you?"

Then the man with the evil spirit attacked the seven sons. He was powerful and tore off their clothes and beat them. Those seven sons ran fast!

The people of Ephesus heard about this. Many believed in Jesus. People who had practiced magic brought their magic books. They burned them before all the people.

These books were worth 50,000 silver coins. This was only one way that the word of the Lord kept spreading and growing stronger.

Diana of the Ephesians

A riot started in Ephesus because of the Christians. This is the way it happened. A silversmith named Demetrius made silver models of the goddess Diana's temple. Sometimes she was called Artemis.

Demetrius made much money from this business. So did other silversmiths who worked with him.

One day Demetrius called his fellow workers together. "You know that we make much money from this business," he told them. "But Paul is hurting our sales. He is also telling people that Diana and her temple are not important."

This made the men angry. "Diana is very important," they shouted. They stirred up a mob and grabbed Gaius and Aristarchus, two of Paul's friends from Macedonia. The mob rushed to the big open theater.

Paul wanted to go there and talk to the mob. But his friends would not let him. A man named Alexander tried to talk, but the mob would not listen to him because he was a Jew. The mob kept shouting, "Diana is great! Diana is great!" They kept doing that for two hours.

At last the city clerk stopped the shouting. "Everyone knows that Ephesus is the center where Diana is worshiped," he said. "So why make such a fuss about it? These men haven't done anything. If Demetrius and his friends have a problem, they should take it to the courts. The judges will do what is right. Or our town meeting can handle it. If the Roman government demands to know why we are rioting, I don't know what to tell them. Now please go home."

So the people went home. The silversmith riot was over.

Eutychus Falls from a Window

Paul was on his way home to Jerusalem. Timothy and some other friends had gone ahead. They had stopped a while at Troas. Then Paul and some other friends joined them five days later and spent a week.

On Saturday night Paul led a communion service. This was in a room on the third floor of a building. The room was lit with many oil lamps, and so the room became quite warm.

Paul preached a long sermon. He kept preaching until midnight. That was the last day he would spend with these people. He had many things to say to them.

A young man named Eutychus was sitting in the large open window. As Paul kept on preaching, Eutychus could hardly stay awake. He fell asleep and dropped to the ground, three stories below.

Everyone rushed downstairs, but Eutychus was dead. Paul went down, too. He took Eutychus in his arms.

"Don't worry," Paul told the Christians. "Eutychus is alive now."

Then everyone went back upstairs. They finished the communion service. But Paul preached again until early morning. Then he left.

Now the people went home. They were certainly happy that Eutychus was alive and well.

Paul Is Arrested

When Paul went back to Jerusalem, he visited the temple. But some people of Asia who hated him saw him there. They began to shout. "Help! This man is doing bad things here in our holy temple," they shouted.

A mob rushed at Paul and dragged him out of the temple. Then the temple doors were closed. The mob began to beat Paul. They wanted to kill him, but some Roman soldiers came and took him away.

The Roman commander put Paul in chains. "Who is he and what has he done?" he asked. But he got many answers. "Away with him," the mob kept shouting. The next day the commander took Paul to the council of religious leaders. He wanted to find why Paul was in trouble. When Paul said he was a Pharisee, the Pharisees were for him, and the Sadducees were against him.

The following day more than 40 men plotted together. They would not eat or drink until they had killed Paul. Paul's nephew, the son of Paul's sister, heard about this and told the army commander.

By nine that night the commander left Jerusalem with 200 soldiers and 70 horsemen and 200 spearmen. They took Paul with them on a horse.

Commander Claudius Lysias sent a letter with Paul and the soldiers. It told Governor Felix at Caesarea why Paul was sent to him.

That night the group camped at Antipatris. The foot soldiers came back to Jerusalem the next day and the others took Paul to Caesarea. They turned Paul over to Governor Felix and went home.

"I will hear you when your accusers come," the governor said. Then he put Paul with guards in the palace built by Herod.

Paul Before Governors and Kings

Paul was in prison in the palace at Caesarea. Five days after he went there Ananias came with other religious leaders. Ananias had been the high priest before his son-in-law Caiaphas.

These men brought an orator named Tertullus. He said that Paul was a troublemaker. He said that Paul was trying to hurt the temple.

Governor Felix let Paul speak next. Paul said he had done nothing wrong. If he did, what was it?

Felix kept Paul guarded after the trial. But he let him have more freedom. He even asked Paul to tell him about Jesus from time to time. After two long years, Porcius Festus became governor in place of Felix.

Festus had another trial. Again the religious leaders from Jerusalem came. Again they spoke lies about Paul. "Will you go to Jerusalem to be tried?" Festus asked.

"No, I want Caesar to judge me," Paul answered. He knew he would not get a fair trial in Jerusalem with those men.

Since Paul was a Roman citizen, he could ask Caesar to judge him. So Festus agreed to let him go to Rome to see Caesar.

A few days later King Agrippa and Bernice came to Caesarea. Agrippa wanted to hear Paul. So Paul was brought before him. When Agrippa heard Paul he said, "He has done nothing wrong. He could be set free if he had not asked to go to Caesar."

Plans were made to send Paul to Rome. There he would be tried by the Roman Emperor, who was called Caesar.

Paul Sails and Is Shipwrecked

aul had asked Caesar, the Roman Emperor, to judge him. He knew he would not get a fair trial in Jerusalem. The religious leaders there hated him. So plans were made to send Paul to Rome.

Julius, an officer in the emperor's army, guarded Paul and some other prisoners. Julius was kind to Paul. When the ship came to Sidon, he let Paul visit friends. They gave Paul what he needed for his trip.

But sailing was hard. The wind was blowing toward the ship. It took much longer than they thought. By the time the ship reached Fair Havens, on the island of Crete, it was getting too late to sail. The sea would soon be dangerous.

One day a strong "Northeaster" wind blew. It blew them far off course. For 14 days the storm kept up. All 276 men on the ship thought they would die.

One night the ship came near land. The sailors put out the anchors. They threw all the grain from the ship into the sea. Then they waited for morning.

When morning came the sailors saw land. They cut the ropes to the anchors. They sailed for the land. But the ship hit a sandbar and broke into pieces. Some men swam to shore. Others floated on boards.

It was raining and cold when the men came to land, an island called Malta. The people built a fire to warm the men.

Suddenly a poisonous snake came from some sticks and bit Paul. When he did not die the people thought he was a god. The shipwrecked people stayed three months on this island. An important man named Publius took care of them. Paul healed Publius's father. He also healed others on the island. So the people were kind to Paul and the other men. They gave them all they needed.

Paul at Rome

A ship from Alexandria had stayed at Malta for the winter. When it was time to go, this ship took Paul and the others toward Rome. They landed at a port called Puteoli. From there Paul would be taken to Rome on one of the Roman roads.

Some Christians came to meet Paul. They asked Paul to stay with them for a week. Then they went on toward Rome. When they were about 40 miles from Rome, some Christians from Rome came to meet them. This was a place called the Appii Forum. Others joined them at a place called the Three Inns. Paul thanked God for these Christians. He felt much better when he saw them.

In Rome, Paul was allowed to live by himself, but he had a Roman guard with him at all times. Many people came to see him. He told them about Jesus.

Three days after Paul arrived, he invited the Jewish leaders in Rome to meet with him. He told them about Jesus and showed them how the Old Testament was about Him. Some of them became Christians. Others would not believe.

For two years, Paul lived in Rome, waiting for his trial. While he was there, he told many people the good news about Jesus. He had great courage and did not worry about getting into trouble. And no one kept him from teaching and preaching about Jesus.

Index